OLIVIA NEWTON-JOHN
All The Top 40 Hits

Craig Halstead

Copyright © Craig Halstead 2018

All rights reserved. No part of this publication may be reproduced, stored in a retrieval system, or transmitted in any form or by any means, electronic, mechanical, photocopy, recording or otherwise, without prior written permission of the copyright owner. Nor can it be circulated in any form of binding or cover other than that in which it is published and without similar condition including this condition being imposed on a subsequent purchaser.

Second Edition

By the same author:

Christmas Number Ones
ABBA: All The Top 40 Hits
Carpenters: All The Top 40 Hits
Janet Jackson: All The Top 40 Hits
Michael Jackson: All The Top 40 Hits
Michael, Janet & The Jacksons: All The Top 40 Singles
Michael, Janet & The Jacksons: All The Top 40 Albums & Music Videos
Donna Summer: For The Record
Whitney Houston: For The Record

With Chris Cadman:

Janet Jackson: For The Record
Michael Jackson: For The Record
Michael Jackson – The Early Years
Michael Jackson – The Solo Years

Fiction:

Tyranny
The Secret Library (James Harris 1)
Shadow Of Death (James Harris 2)
Cataclysm Book 1: The First 73 Days
Cataclysm Book 2: A New Year

www.craighalstead.com

for Aaron

ACKNOWLEDGEMENTS

I would like to thank Chris Cadman, my writing partner, for helping to make my writing dreams come true. It's incredible to think how far we have come, since we got together to compile 'The Complete Michael Jackson Discography 1972-1990', for Adrian Grant's *Off the Wall* fan magazine in 1990. Good luck with 'Off The Wall For The Record', Chris ~ I'm sure you will have another winner on your hands!

I would like to thank the online music community, who so readily share and exchange information at: ukmix (ukmix.org/forums), Haven (fatherandy2.proboards.com) & Buzzjack (buzzjack.com/forums). In particular, I would like to thank:

- 'BrainDamagell' & 'Wayne' for posting current Canadian charts on ukmix;
- 'flatdeejay' & 'ChartFreaky' for posting German chart action, and 'Indi' for answering my queries regarding Germany, on ukmix;
- 'mario' for posting Japanese chart action, and 'danavon' for answering my queries regarding Japan, on ukmix;
- 'Davidalic' for posting Spanish chart action on ukmix;
- 'Shakyfan', 'CZB', 'trebor' & 'beatlened' for posting Irish charts on ukmix;
- 'grendizer' for posting Canadian certifications on ukmix;
- 'Hanboo' for posting and up-dating on request full UK & USA chart runs on ukmix.

R.I.P., Hanboo ~ like everyone on ukmix, I was shocked and deeply saddened to learn of your passing.

If you can fill any of the gaps in the chart information in this book, or have chart runs from a country not already featured in the book, I would love to hear from you. You can contact me via **www.craighalstead.com** ~ thank you!

CONTENTS

INTRODUCTION   7
- Including the Charts
(Australia, Austria, Canada, Germany, Ireland, Japan, Netherlands, New Zealand, Norway, South Africa, Spain, Sweden, Switzerland, United Kingdom, United States of America)

ALL THE TOP 40 SINGLES   13

THE ALMOST TOP 40 SINGLES   103

THE TOP 20 OLIVIA SINGLES   104

SINGLES TRIVIA   107

ALL THE TOP 40 ALBUMS   119

THE ALMOST TOP 40 ALBUMS   201

THE TOP 20 OLIVIA ALBUMS   202

ALBUMS TRIVIA   203

INTRODUCTION

Olivia Newton-John was born in Cambridge, England, on 26th September 1948. She was the third and youngest child of a Welsh father, Brinley Newton-John, and a German mother, Irene Helene (neé Born), and followed a son Hugh and a daughter Rona.

Olivia's maternal grandfather, Max Born, won the Nobel Prize for Physics in 1954 – the same year Olivia and her family emigrated to Melbourne, Australia. Eight years later, when she was 14, Olivia and three friends formed a short-lived female quartet called Sol Four.

By the time she was 16, Olivia was a regular on local radio, and she had appeared on several TV shows, often performing as 'Lovely Livvy'. On one show, *Go Show*, she met John Farrar and his wife-to-be Pat Carroll, who went on to become Olivia's producer and duet partner, respectively.

In 1964, Olivia was a contestant on the TV talent show *Sing, Sing, Sing*. She performed two songs, *Anyone Who Had A Heart* and *Everything's Coming Up Roses*, and although she won initially she was reluctant to take up her prize: a trip to the United Kingdom. So reluctant, it wasn't until 1966 that she finally gave in to her mother's encouragement, and boarded a ship.

Later the same year, Olivia released her debut single on Decca Records, *Till You Say You'll Be Mine* b/w *Forever*, but it wasn't a hit.

Homesick, Olivia booked several trips back to Australia, only to have her mother cancel them. She finally settled when Pat Carroll joined her in the UK, and together they formed a duo, Pat & Olivia, performing at nightclubs in the UK and Europe until Pat's visa expired, and she returned to Australia.

brujula
OLIVIA NEWTON-JOHN
TOOMORROW
TOOMORROW
in
mañana
con BENNY THOMAS - VIC COOPER - KARL CHAMBERS - ROY DOTRICE
Director: VAL GUEST
Música compuesta y dirigida por: HUGO MONTENEGRO

In 1970, Olivia was recruited by American producer Don Kirshner, to join the group Toomorrow. The group starred in a low budget science fiction musical and released a soundtrack album, but both flopped and the group disbanded.

The following year, Olivia released her debut solo album, *IF NOT FOR YOU*, and the Bob Dylan-penned title track became her first hit single. Another track from the album, *Banks Of The Ohio*, was also a hit single.

A string of hit singles and albums followed then, in 1978, Olivia starred in her second film, *Grease* – which went on to become one of the most successful musicals ever.

All The Top 40 Hits

For the purposes of this book, to qualify as a Top 40 hit, a single or album must have entered the Top 40 singles/albums chart in at least one of the following featured countries: Australia, Austria, Canada, Germany, Ireland (singles only), Japan, Netherlands, New Zealand, Norway, South Africa, Spain, Sweden, Switzerland, United Kingdom and United States of America.

The Top 40 singles and albums are detailed chronologically, according to the date they first entered the chart in one or more of the featured countries. Each Top 40 single and album is illustrated and the catalogue numbers and release dates are detailed, for both Australia and the UK, followed by the chart runs in each featured country, including any chart re-entries. Where full chart runs are unavailable, peak position and weeks on the chart are given.

For both singles and albums, the main listing is followed by 'The Almost Top 40 Singles/Albums', which gives an honorable mention to Olivia's singles/albums that peaked between no.41 and no.50 in one or more countries. There is also a points-based list of the Olivia's most successful singles and albums, plus a fascinating 'Trivia' section at the end of each section which looks at the most successful of Olivia's singles and albums in each of the featured countries.

The Charts

The charts from an increasing number of countries are now freely available online, and for many countries it is possible to research weekly chart runs. Although this book focuses on Top 40 hits, longer charts runs are included where available, up to the Top 100 for countries where a Top 100 or longer is published. Where full chart runs are unavailable, peak positions and weeks on the chart are detailed.

Nowadays, charts are compiled and published on a weekly basis – in the past, however, some countries published charts on a bi-weekly or monthly basis, and most charts listed far fewer titles than they do today. There follows a summary of the current charts from each country featured in this book, together with relevant online resources and chart books.

Australia
Current charts: Top 100 Singles & Top 100 Albums.
Online resources: current weekly Top 50 Singles & Albums, but no archive, at **ariacharts.com.au**; archive of complete weekly charts dating back to 2001 at **pandora.nla.gov.au/tep/23790**; searchable archive of Top 50 Singles & Albums dating back to 1988 at **australian-charts.com**.
Books: 'Australian Chart Book 1970-1992' & 'Australian Chart Book 1993-2009' by David Kent.

Austria
Current charts: Top 75 Singles & Top 75 Albums.
Online resources: current weekly charts and a searchable archive dating back to 1965 for singles and 1973 for albums at **austriancharts.at**.

Canada
Current charts: Hot 100 Singles & Top 100 Albums.
Online resources: weekly charts and a searchable archive of weekly charts from the Nielsen SoundScan era at **billboard.com/biz** (subscription only); weekly charts are posted on **ukmix.org**; incomplete archive of weekly RPM charts dating back to 1964 for singles and 1967 for albums at **collectionscanada.gc.ca/rpm** (RPM folded in 2000).
Book: 'The Canadian Singles Chart Book 1975-1996' by Nanda Lwin.

Germany
Current charts: Top 100 Singles & Top 100 Albums.
Online resources: current weekly charts (Top 10s only) and a searchable archive dating back to 2007 (again, Top 10s only) at **germancharts.com**; complete Top 100 charts are usually posted weekly in the German Charts Thread on **ukmix.org**.
Books: *'Deutsche Chart Singles 1956-1980'*, *'Deutsche Chart Singles 1981-90'*, *'Deutsche Chart Singles 1991-1995'* & *'Deutsche Chart LP's 1962-1986'* published by Taurus Press.

Ireland
Current charts: Top 100 Singles & Top 100 Albums.
Online resources: current weekly charts are published at IRMA (**irma.ie**); there is a searchable archive for Top 30 singles (entry date, peak position and week on chart only) at **irishcharts.ie**; an annual Irish Chart Thread has been published annually from 2007 to date, plus singles charts from 1967 to 1999 and album charts for 1993, 1995-6 and 1999, have been published at ukmix (**ukmix.org**); weekly album charts from March 2003 to date can be found at **acharts.us/ireland_albums_top_75**.
Note: the information presented in this book is for singles only.

Japan
Current charts: Top 200 Singles & Top 300 Albums.
Online resources: current weekly charts (in Japanese) at **oricon.co.jp/rank**; selected information is available on the Japanese Chart/The Newest Charts and Japanese Chart/The Archives threads at **ukmix.org**.

Netherlands
Current charts: Top 100 Singles & Top 100 Albums.
Online resources: current weekly charts and a searchable archive dating back to 1956 for singles and 1969 for albums at **dutchcharts.nl**.

New Zealand
Current charts: Top 40 Singles & Top 40 Albums.
Online resources: current weekly charts and a searchable archive dating back to 1975 at **charts.org.nz**.
Book: 'The Complete New Zealand Music Charts 1966-2006' by Dean Scapolo.

Norway
Current charts: Top 20 Singles & Top 40 Albums.
Online resources: current weekly charts and a searchable archive dating back to 1958 for singles and 1967 for albums at **norwegiancharts.com**.

South Africa
Current charts: no official charts.
Online resources: none known.
Book: 'South Africa Chart Book' by Christopher Kimberley.
Notes: the singles chart was discontinued in early 1989, as singles were no longer being manufactured in significant numbers. The albums chart only commenced in December 1981, and was discontinued in 1995, following re-structuring of the South African Broadcasting Corporation.

Spain
Current charts: Top 50 Singles & Top 100 Albums.
Online resources: current weekly charts and a searchable archive dating back to 2005 at **spanishcharts.com**.
Book: *'Sólo éxitos 1959-2002 Año a Año'* by Fernando Salaverri.

Sweden
Current charts: Top 60 Singles & Top 100 Albums.
Online resources: current weekly charts and a searchable archive dating back to 1975 at **swedishcharts.com**.

Note: before 1975, a weekly Top 20 *Kvällstoppen* charts was published, which was a sales-based, mixed singles/albums chart.

Switzerland
Current charts: Top 75 Singles & Top 100 Albums.
Online resources: current weekly charts and a searchable archive dating back to 1968 for singles and 1983 for albums at **hitparade.ch**.

UK
Current Charts: Top 100 Singles & Top 200 Albums.
Online resources: current weekly Top 100 charts and a searchable archive dating back to 1960 at **officialcharts.com**; weekly charts are posted on a number of music forums, including ukmix (**ukmix.org**), Haven (**fatherandy2.proboards.com**) and Buzzjack (**buzzjack.com**).
Note: starting in January 1989, various artist albums – including soundtracks like *GREASE* and *XANADU* – were excluded from the UK's Top 100 Albums chart, and were consigned to a separate Compilations chart. The information presented in this book relates to the main albums chart only. Weekly Top 200 albums charts are only available via subscription from UK ChartsPlus (**ukchartsplus.co.uk**).

USA
Current charts: Hot 100 Singles & Billboard 200 Albums.
Online resources: current weekly charts are available at **billboard.com**, however, to access Billboard's searchable archive at **billboard.com/biz** you must be a subscriber; weekly charts are posted on a number of music forums, including ukmix (**ukmix.org**), Haven (**fatherandy2.proboards.com**) and Buzzjack (**buzzjack.com**).
Note: older 'catalog' albums (i.e. albums older than two years) were excluded from the Billboard 200 before December 2009, so the chart didn't accurately reflect the country's best-selling albums. Therefore, in this book Billboard's Top Comprehensive Albums chart has been used from December 2003 to December 2009, as this did include all albums. In December 2009 the Top Comprehensive Albums chart became the Billboard 200, and Billboard launched a new Top Current Albums chart – effectively, the old Billboard 200.

Note: In the past, there was often one or more weeks over Christmas and New Year when no new album chart was published in some countries. In such cases, the previous week's chart has been used to complete a chart run. Similarly, where a bi-weekly or monthly chart was in place, for chart runs these are counted at two and four weeks, respectively.

All The Top 40 Singles

1 ~ IF NOT FOR YOU

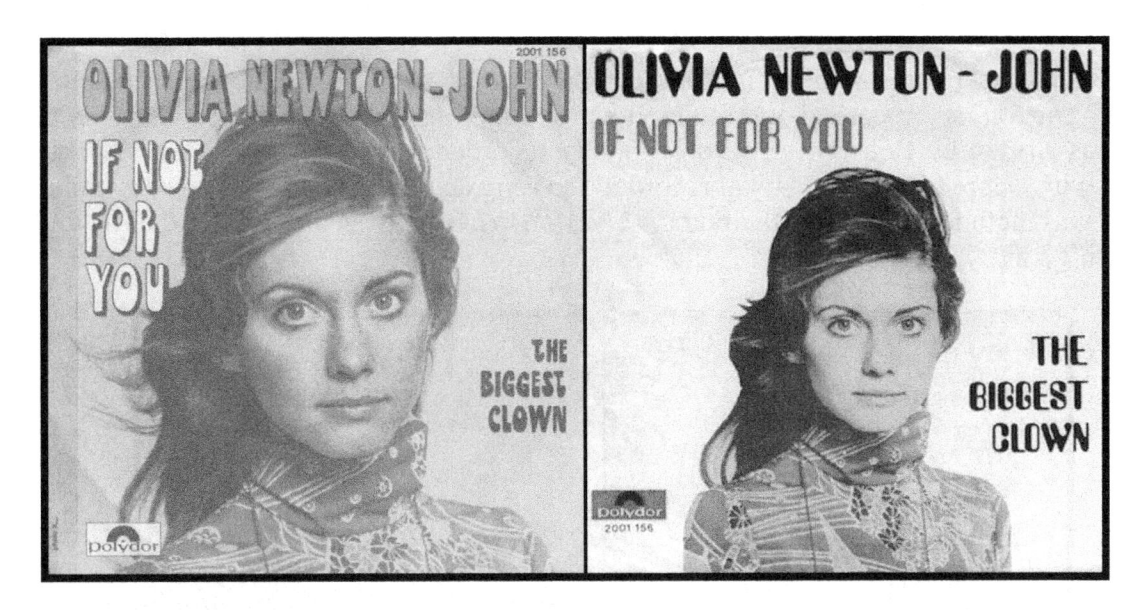

Australia: Interfusion ITFK-4158 (1971).
  B-side: *The Biggest Clown*.

26.04.71: peaked at no.**7**, charted for 19 weeks.

UK: Pye International 7N.25543 (1971).
  B-side: *The Biggest Clown*.

20.03.71: 24-22-12-12-8-**7**-11-14-29-33-39

Canada
15.05.71: 98-85-75-72-61-58-43-43-39-38-38-38-26-25-23-21-**18**-24-30-54-100

Ireland
1.05.71: 8-**6**-8-15

New Zealand
9.07.71: peaked at no.**8**, charted for 6 weeks

Norway
29.05.71: 9-8-9-9-7-7-**6-6-6-6**-10-10

USA
29.05.71: 98-89-81-76-63-51-48-37-36-34-33-31-27-26-**25**-29-32

Olivia released her debut single, *Till You Say You'll Be Mine*, in 1966 but it wasn't a hit.

Five years on, she recorded and released her debut album, *IF NOT FOR YOU*. The title track was written by Bob Dylan, who originally recorded the song on 1st May 1970, in a session with George Harrison. Dylan recorded the song again on 12th August 1970, and this version was included on his 1970 album, *NEW MORNING*. It was also released as a single, but wasn't a hit.

Later the same year, George Harrison recorded a version of *If Not For You* for his triple album, *ALL THINGS MUST PASS*, but it wasn't issued as a single.

Dylan's original recording of *If Not For You* remained unreleased until 1991, when it was included on *THE BOOTLEG SERIES VOLUMES 1-3 – RARE & UNRELEASED*.

Olivia's recording of *If Not For You* was based on Harrison's, rather than Dylan's, arrangement of the song. However, not convinced the song would suit her, Olivia had to be persuaded to record it by Bruce Welch and John Farrar. 'I didn't think it was my type of song at all,' she admitted, 'and I had a little bit of trouble being convincing in putting it over. But everyone else was so enthusiastic that I came round to liking it eventually.'

Issued as the lead single from the album with the same title, *If Not For You* became Olivia's first hit, charting at no.6 in Ireland and Norway, no.7 in Australia and the UK, no.8 in New Zealand and no.25 in the USA.

2 ~ BANKS OF THE OHIO

Australia: Interfusion ITFK-4397 (1971).
  B-side: *Love Song*.

27.09.71: peaked at no.**1** (5 weeks), charted for 25 weeks

UK: Pye International 7N.25568 (1971).
  B-side: *Would You Follow Me*.

23.10.71: 49-29-21-11-**6**-8-7-6-9-9-11-22-23-29-34-38-49

Germany
24.01.72: 47-x-x-35-33-**13**-21-18-15-42-24-40-41

Ireland
11.11.71: 18-11-10-**9**-12-12-?-?

New Zealand
19.11.71: peaked at no.**3**, charted for 11 weeks

USA
16.10.71: 98-95-95-**94**

Dating from the 19th century, *Down By The Banks Of The Ohio*, as it was originally titled, is known as a 'murder ballad', but it is not known who composed it.

The ballad was recorded by numerous country artists during the 1920s and 1930s, with the earliest known recording by Red Patterson's Piedmont Log Rollers dating to 1927. A 1936 recording by Blue Sky Boys featured in the 1973 film, *Paper Moon*.

Olivia often performed *Banks Of The Ohio* live in concert, prior to recording it for her debut album, *IF NOT FOR YOU*, with an arrangement by John Farrar and Bruce Welch.

Issued as the follow-up to *If Not For You*, *Banks Of The Ohio* went all the way to no.1 in Australia, and charted at no.3 in New Zealand, no.6 in the UK, no.9 in Ireland and no.13 in Germany, but it was only a minor hit in the USA.

3 ~ WHAT IS LIFE

Australia: Interfusion ITFK-4577 (1972).
  B-side: *I'm A Small And Lonely Light*.

What Is Life wasn't a hit in Australia.

UK: Pye International 7N.25575 (1972).
  B-side: *I'm A Small And Lonely Light*.

11.03.72: 47-34-21-20-**16**-18-17-41

Ireland
1.04.72: **18**

What Is Life was written by George Harrison in 1969, originally for Billy Preston, but he subsequently recorded the song himself in late May/early June the following year, for inclusion on his album *ALL THINGS MUST PASS*.
  Released as a single in most countries, *What Is Life* hit no.1 in Switzerland, and achieved Top 10 status in several other countries, including Austria, Belgium, Canada, France, New Zealand, Netherlands, Norway and the USA.
  In the UK, where Harrison declined to release a single from *ALL THINGS MUST PASS* until January 1971, *What Is Life* was issued as the B-side to *My Sweet Lord*, which went all the way to no.1 and became one of the biggest selling singles of the year globally.

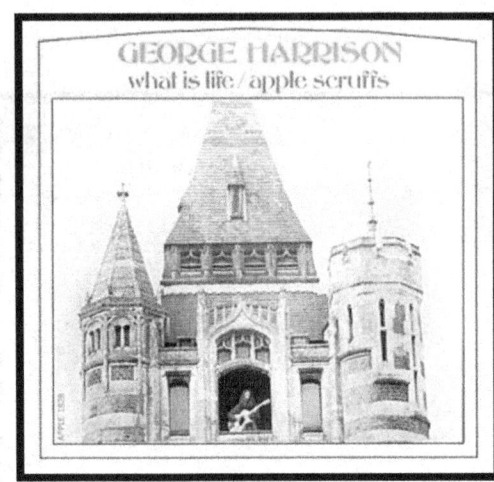

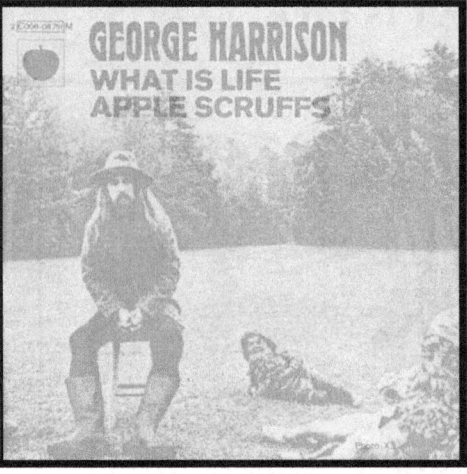

What Is Life is one of two songs from Harrison's *ALL THINGS MUST PASS* album that Olivia recorded for her 1972 album, *OLIVIA*, the second being *Behind That Locked Door*.

Given the success of Harrison's original, Olivia's cover of *What Is Life* was only released in a limited number of countries, and was only a hit in two, the UK and Ireland, where it achieved no.16 and no.18, respectively.

4 ~ TAKE ME HOME COUNTRY ROADS

Australia: Interfusion ITFK-4939 (1972).
  B-side: *Sail Into Tomorrow*.

Take Me Home Country Roads wasn't a hit in Australia.

UK: Pye International 7N.25599 (1972).
  B-side: *Sail Into Tomorrow*.

13.01.73: 50-35-33-27-18-18-**15**-17-22-26-31-37-35

Ireland
22.02.73: 17-x-15-**5-5**-6-8-13-x-19

Japan
2.10.76: peaked at no.**6**, charted for 31 weeks

Take Me Home, Country Roads was originally composed by Bill Danoff and Taffy Nivert, who whilst travelling to Maryland for a family reunion were inspired by the winding roads and West Virginia countryside. They intended trying to sell the song to Johnny Cash.
  As the duo Fat City, Danoff & Nivert were playing as the opening act for John Denver at The Cellar Door, Washington D.C., in a series of gigs that kicked off on 22nd December

1970. One evening, following the concert, Danoff & Nivert played *Take Me Home, Country Roads* for Denver, and in his words 'I flipped!'

Denver, Danoff & Nivert stayed up all night, re-working the lyrics, and it was agreed that instead of trying to sell it Denver could record the song for his forthcoming album. Denver premiered the song at The Cellar Door on 30th December, and was rewarded with a five minute standing ovation. He went on to record the song for his 1971 album, *POEMS, PRAYERS & PROMISES*.

The original pressings of *Take Me Home, Country Roads* as a single credited 'John Denver with Fat City'. The single was massively popular in North America, rising to no.2 in the USA and no.3 in Canada, but it failed to enter the charts in most countries.

Olivia recorded *Take Me Home Country Roads* (with the comma between 'Home' and 'Country' usually dropped) for her 1973 album, *LET ME BE THERE*. Released as a single, the song charted at no.5 in Ireland, no.6 in Japan and no.15 in the UK.

Take Me Home, Country Roads has been covered by numerous artists over the years, including Lynn Anderson, Ray Charles, Skeeter Davis and Loretta Lynn.

5 ~ LET ME BE THERE

Australia: Interfusion K-5189 (1973).
  B-side: *Maybe Then I'll Think Of You.*

24.09.73: peaked at no.**11**, charted for 30 weeks

UK: Pye International 7N 25618 (1973).
  B-side: *Maybe Then I'll Think Of You.*

Let Me Be There wasn't a hit in the UK.

Canada
3.11.73: 91-85-84
12.01.74: 51-33-19-13-6-**5-5**-11-21-25

New Zealand
14.12.73: peaked at no.**8**, charted for 13 weeks

USA
17.11.73: 87-77-60-44-31-24-17-13-9-9-8-7-**6**-7-10-15-25-39-52

Let Me Be There was written by John Rostill, and unlike her previous hit singles which were all covers, Olivia was the first artist to record the song.

The title of her 1973 album, *Let Me Be There* gave Olivia her first Top 10 single in the USA, where it peaked at no.6. The single went Top 3 in Canada, and charted at no.8 in New Zealand and no.11 in Australia, but it wasn't a success in Europe.

Elvis Presley recorded a live version of *Let Me Be There*, which was released on his 1974 album, *RECORDED LIVE ON STAGE IN MEMPHIS*, and he often performed the song in concert.

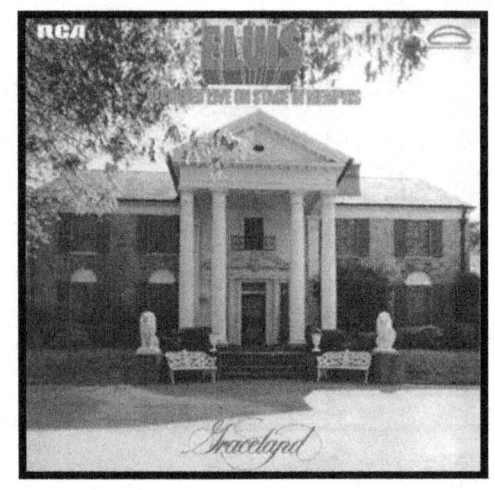

Olivia was honoured with her first Grammy Award for *Let Me Be There*, for Best Country Vocalist, Female.

6 ~ LONG LIVE LOVE

Australia: Interfusion K-5505 (1974).
B-side: *Angel Eyes*.

10.06.74: peaked at no.**11**, charted for 22 weeks

UK: Pye International 7N 25638 (1974).
B-side: *Angel Eyes*.

16.03.74: 28-21-18-16-**11**-19-22-49

Ireland
28.03.74: 15-**9**-14-14-17

Norway
27.04.74: **3-3-3**-4-5-5-5-5-5-6-6-7

Long Live Love was composed by Valerie Avon and Harold Spiro. It was one of six nominated songs Olivia performed, over six weeks, on Jimmy Saville's *Clunk Click* TV show, as contenders for the UK's entry to the 19th annual Eurovision Song Contest.
When the results of a public vote were announced on *A Song For Europe 1974*, on 23rd February 1974, *Long Live Love* was the clear winner with 27,387 votes. Olivia's personal

favourite, *Angel Eyes*, was the runner-up with 18,018 votes – it was chosen as the B-side, for single release.

The 19th annual Eurovision Song Contest was staged at The Dome in Brighton, England, on 6th April 1974. On the night Olivia and *Long Live Love* finished in joint 4th place, behind the winner *Waterloo* by ABBA, Gigliola Cinquetti's *Si* and Mouth & MacNeal's *I See A Star*. Cinquetti's *Si* was released as *Go (Before You Break My Heart)* in the UK, and all three of the songs that finished ahead of *Long Live Love* were hits in the UK, with *Waterloo* going to no.1.

Long Live Love, although a hit in several countries, wasn't the huge success in Europe that Olivia and her team hoped it would be. The single achieved no.3 in Norway, no.9 in Ireland, and no.11 in Australia and the UK, but missed the charts in most countries.

7 ~ IF YOU LOVE ME (LET ME KNOW)

Australia: Interfusion K-5582 (1974).
  B-side: *Rosewater*.

10.02.75: peaked at no.**2**, charted for 22 weeks

UK: EMI 2180 (1974).
  B-side: *Brotherly Love*.

If You Love Me (Let Me Know) wasn't a Top 50 hit in the UK, however, it did spend five weeks on the 'Bubbling Under' chart, peaking at no.56.

Canada
6.04.74: 100-85-59-50-50-43-36-24-23-15-10-9-**4-4-4-4**-14-22-39

Germany
26.08.74: **37**-47

New Zealand
6.09.74: peaked at no.**10**, charted for 9 weeks

USA
13.04.74: 87-77-62-50-39-31-25-20-15-11-7-**5-5**-12-10-27-42-48-61-80

If You Love Me (Let Me Know), like *Let Me Be There*, was written by John Rostill, and Olivia recorded the song for her 1974 album with the same title (minus the brackets).

The single rose to no.2 in Australia, and gave Olivia her second Top success in the USA, where it peaked at no.5. Elsewhere, the single achieved no.10 in New Zealand and no.37 in Germany, but it narrowly failed to enter the Top 50 in the UK.

If You Love Me (Let Me Know) is another song Elvis Presley was fond of, and often performed live in concert. One such performance was recorded, and released on his 1977 live album, *ELVIS IN CONCERT*.

Rosewater, the B-side of *If You Love Me (Let Me Know)* in some countries, including Australia, is a song Olivia composed herself.

IF YOU LOVE ME
(let me know)
EMI 2180

OLIVIA NEWTON-JOHN

the new single by
OLIVIA NEWTON JOHN
ALREADY A TOP TEN MILLION SELLER IN THE USA
and her latest album

LONG LIVE LOVE

8 ~ I HONESTLY LOVE YOU

Australia: Interfusion K-5660 (1974).
  B-side: *Home Ain't Home Anymore*.

30.09.74: peaked at no.**1** (4 weeks), charted for 23 weeks

UK: MCA MCA-40280 (1974).
  B-side: *Home Ain't Home Anymore*.

12.10.74: 35-29-**22-22**-25-38
8.01.83: 76-54-52-61-75

Canada
24.08.74: 94-58-31-20-11-7-**1**-3-4-4-6-8-8-6-5-36-65
19.11.77: 97-76-62-58-55-55-50-64

New Zealand
15.11.74: peaked at no.**4**, charted for 10 weeks

USA
17.08.74: 63-39-26-19-12-3-2-**1-1**-4-19-42-86-100-100
5.11.77: 85-74-63-52-48-66-69-69-69
30.05.98: 71-69-67-67-71-76-78-86-85-80-90-99 (re-recording)

Originally titled as *I Love You, I Honestly Love You*, *I Honestly Love You* was written by Jeff Barry with Peter Allen, for the latter's new album. But when Olivia heard the song, she loved it so much she asked if she could record it instead. Her version was originally released on her album *LONG LIVE LOVE*, and was later included on *IF YOU LOVE ME LET ME KNOW* in North America, where *LONG LIVE LOVE* wasn't released.

Peter Allen also recorded *I Love You, I Honestly Love You* for his 1974 album, *CONTINENTAL AMERICAN*, and released it as the B-side of his single, *Just Ask Me, I've Been There*.

'No one thought it was going to be a single,' said Jeff Barry, referring to Olivia's version of *I Honestly Love You*. 'The label didn't want to put it out, but radio demanded it.'

Olivia's most successful single to date, *I Honestly Love You* hit no.1 in Australia, Canada and the USA, and charted at no.4 in New Zealand and no.22 in the UK. The single went Platinum in the USA, where it sold over two million copies, and picked up two prestigious awards at the 17th annual Grammy Awards, staged at the Uris Theater, New York, on 1st March 1975:

- Record Of The Year
- Best Pop Vocal Performance, Female

I Honestly Love You was re-released in North America in 1977, and re-entered the chart, rising to no.48 in the USA and no.50 in Canada. Six years later, the single was reissued in the UK to promote Olivia's *GREATEST HITS* compilation, and charted at no.52.

Olivia re-recorded *I Honestly Love You* in 1998, with Kenneth 'Babyface' Edmonds on backing vocals, for her album *BACK WITH A HEART*, but only a minor hit resulted.

9 ~ HAVE YOU NEVER BEEN MELLOW

Australia: Interfusion K-5821 (1975).
  B-side: *Water Under The Bridge*.

7.04.75: peaked at no.**10**, charted for 20 weeks

UK: EMI 2271 (1975).
  B-side: *Water Under The Bridge*.

Have You Never Been Mellow wasn't a hit in the UK.

Canada
8.02.75: 88-33-15-5-**1-1-1**-2-6-12-15-21-41-41-41-44

Japan
5.04.75: peaked at no.**26**, charted for 20 weeks

New Zealand
9.05.75: **12**-14-18-18-23-23-22-20-23-26-26-26-35-33

USA
25.01.75: 63-49-34-18-5-2-**1**-4-5-10-9-19-31-56-68-81

Have You Never Been Mellow was composed by John Farrar, Olivia's producer, and was released as the lead single from her 1975 album with the same title.

Like *I Honestly Love You*, *Have You Never Been Mellow* went to no.1 in both Canada and the USA, but it was less successful in Australia, where it peaked at no.10. The single also achieved no.12 in New Zealand and no.26 in Japan, but missed the charts in most countries, including the UK.

In the USA, *Have You Never Been Mellow* was nominated for a Grammy Award, for Best Pop Vocal Performance, Female, but this time Olivia lost out to Janis Ian's *At Seventeen*.

10 ~ PLEASE MR. PLEASE

Australia: Interfusion K-5992 (1975).
  B-side: *And In The Morning*.

11.08.75: peaked at no.**35**, charted for 16 weeks

UK: EMI 2723 (1975).
  B-side: *Don't Cry For Me Argentina*.

Please Mr. Please wasn't a hit in the UK.

Canada
7.06.75: 98-76-64-38-21-17-10-5-2-**1**-8-12-21-29-33-43-47

New Zealand
15.08.75: 40-12-13-13-10-**7**-9-15-19-17-34-27-38-38

USA
7.06.75: 65-46-34-15-10-6-5-4-4-**3**-**3**-10-31-37-57

Please Mr. Please was composed by Bruce Welch and John Rostill, at the time both members of The Shadows, who backed Cliff Richard on most of his early hits, and scored many instrumental hits in their own right.

Bruce Welch recorded a solo version of *Please Mr. Please* in 1974, but his version of the song wasn't a hit anywhere.

Olivia recorded *Please Mr. Please* for her album *HAVE YOU NEVER BEEN MELLOW*, and in most countries it was released as the follow-up to the title track.

Please Mr. Please gave Olivia a hat-trick of no.1 singles in Canada, but it peaked at no.3 in the USA, no.7 in New Zealand and a lowly no.35 in Australia. Elsewhere, including the UK, the single wasn't a hit.

11 ~ SOMETHING BETTER TO DO

Australia: Interfusion K-6149 (1975).
  B-side: *He's My Rock*.

1.12.75: peaked at no.**60**, charted for 13 weeks

UK: EMI 2356 (1975).
  B-side: *He's My Rock*.

Something Better To Do wasn't a hit in the UK.

Canada
27.09.75: 88-80-72-50-42
13.12.75: 34-**26**-57

Japan
5.11.75: peaked at no.**87**, charted for 4 weeks

New Zealand
13.02.76: **40**

USA
20.09.75: 77-66-52-19-17-15-**13**-**13**-17-31-47

Something Better To Do was written by John Farrar, and was chosen as the lead single from Olivia's 1975 album, *CLEARLY LOVE*.

Although it gave Olivia her fifth no.1 on Billboard's Easy Listening chart, *Something Better To Do* broke her run of five consecutive Top 10 singles on the Hot 100 in the USA, where it peaked at no.13.

The single achieved no.26 in Canada and no.40 in New Zealand, but charted outside the Top 40 in Australia and Japan, and wasn't a hit in most countries including, once again, the UK.

12 ~ LET IT SHINE / HE AIN'T HEAVY ... HE'S MY BROTHER

Australia: Interfusion K-6228 (1975).
  B-side: *He Ain't Heavy ... He's My Brother*.

Let It Shine wasn't a hit in Australia.

UK: Not Released.

Canada
27.12.75: 20-20-19-**17**-26-39-47-47-53-68-87

USA
6.12.75: 75-63-53-43-36-34-**30-30**-62

Let It Shine was composed by Linda Hargrove, who recorded the song for her 1973 album, *MUSIC IS YOUR MISTRESS*, while *He Ain't Heavy, He's My Brother* was written by Bobby Scott and Bob Russell in 1969, and became a global hit later the same year for The Hollies.
  Olivia recorded both songs for her 1975 album, *CLEARLY LOVE*, and they were released as the follow-up to *Something Better To Do*, with *Let It Shine* initially as the B-side. The single achieved no.17 in Canada and no.30 in the USA, where *He Ain't Heavy ... He's My Brother* was listed alongside *Let It Shine On* the Hot 100.

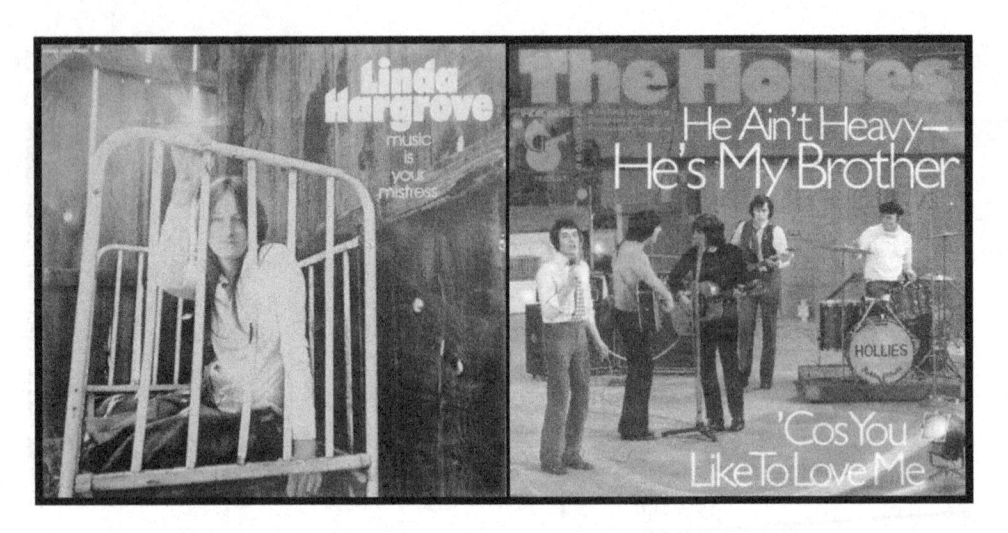

Let It Shine failed to enter the charts in Australia and New Zealand, and in the UK – where Olivia's most recent singles all missed the chart – *Let It Shine* wasn't even released.

FLY AWAY

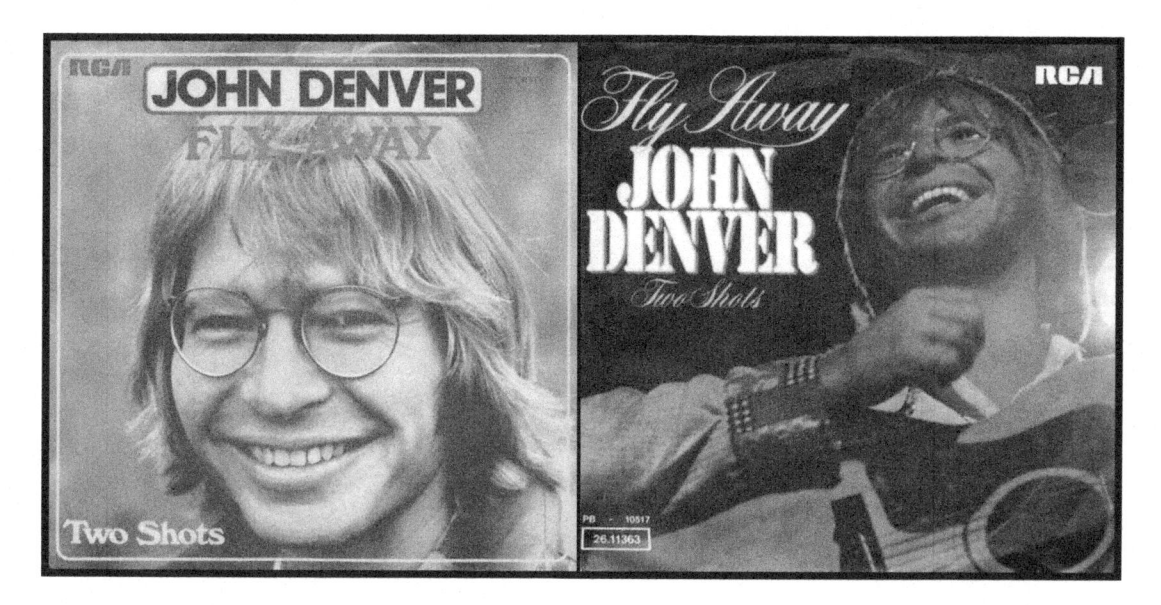

Australia: RCA Victor 102721 (1975).
  B-side: *Two Shots*.

Fly Away wasn't a hit in Australia.

UK: RCA Victor 2646 (1975).
  B-side: *Two Shots*.

Fly Away wasn't a hit in the UK.

Canada
20.12.75: 81-45-45-31-18-**13**-21-26-36-52-57-69-92

USA
6.12.75: 58-37-29-23-18-16-14-**13**-**13**-37-59-59

Fly Away was written and recorded by John Denver, with Olivia contributing uncredited backing vocals, for his 1975 album, *WINDSONG*. The album went to no.1 in both Australia and the USA.
  Released as a single, *Fly Away* rose to no.13 in Canada and the USA, but it failed to chart in most countries, including Australia and the UK.

13 ~ COME ON OVER

Australia: Interfusion K-6330 (1976).
  B-side: *Small Talk And Pride*.

17.05.76: peaked at no.**55**, charted for 13 weeks

UK: EMI 2466 (1976).
  B-side: *Small Talk And Pride*.

Come On Over wasn't a hit in the UK.

Canada
27.03.76: 94-70-33-26-**22**-27-33-45-48-54

Japan
1.04.76: **94**

New Zealand
11.06.76: 20-17-13-14-7-5-9-6-**3**-5-5-7-9-12-16-17-14-28-32-33-32-40

USA
13.03.76: 83-70-60-50-45-36-35-29-**23**-**23**-36-58

Barry and Robin Gibb composed *Come On Over*, and recorded it with their brother Maurice for the 1975 Bee Gees album, *MAIN COURSE*. In the USA, *Come On Over* was also released as the B-side of the hit single, *Jive Talkin'*.

Olivia recorded a cover of *Come On Over* for her 1976 album with the same title, and it was released as the album's lead single.

Come On Over was a big hit in New Zealand, where it rose to no.3, but it was less successful in other countries, charting at no.22 in Canada and no.23 in the USA. The single peaked outside the Top 40 in Australia, was a minor hit in Japan, but continued Olivia's run of chart misses in the UK.

14 ~ JOLENE

Australia: Interfusion K7058 (1976).
  B-side: *Changes*.

10.04.78: peaked at no.**29**, charted for 30 weeks

UK: Not Released.

Japan
5.08.76: peaked at no.**11**, charted for 37 weeks

Jolene was written and originally recorded by Dolly Parton in 1973, and was included on her 1974 album with the same title.

Released as a single towards the end of 1973, *Jolene* was only a minor hit on Billboard's Hot 100 for Parton, but when it was issued in the UK in 1976, it achieved no.7 in the UK and no.8 in Ireland.

In the USA, Olivia's recent singles had done well on Billboard's Country chart, as well as the Hot 100, and she was voted the 1974 Female Vocalist of the Year by the Country Music Association, ahead of established country stars Anne Murray, Dolly Parton, Loretta Lynne and Tanya Tucker. The award proved hugely controversial with critics, and with country music performers and fans alike.

'Some of them weren't too thrilled with this imposter, this outsider,' Olivia acknowledged, 'this Australian person from England. They couldn't quite figure me out.'

Initially, Dolly Parton was one of the artists who sided with the traditionalists, but then she changed her mind and spoke out in support of Olivia, and encouraged her to ignore all the fuss. Olivia recorded a cover of Parton's *Jolene* for her 1976 album, *COME ON OVER*, as a way of thanking her for her support.

Jolene became Olivia's most successful single in Japan, where it charted at no.11. The single also achieved no.29 in Australia, but in many countries – including the UK where Parton's original was a Top 10 hit – it was passed over for single release.

15 ~ DON'T STOP BELIEVIN'

Australia: Interfusion K-6520 (1976).
  B-side: *Greensleeves*.

25.10.76: peaked at no.**93**, charted for 3 weeks

UK: EMI 2519 (1976).
  B-side: *Greensleeves*.

Don't Stop Believin' wasn't a hit in the UK.

Canada
14.08.76: 99-84-75-63-42-**37**-42-47-54

Ireland
22.09.76: 18-18-**17**-22

New Zealand
17.12.76: **34**
13.02.77: 39

USA
7.08.76: 80-70-57-47-39-35-**33**-39-75

Don't Stop Believin' was written by John Farrar, and recorded by Olivia for her 1976 album with the same title.

Released as the lead single, *Don't Stop Believin'* did particularly well in Ireland, where it charted at no.17. The single also achieved Top 40 status in the USA, New Zealand and Canada, where it peaked at no.33, no.34 and no.37, respectively.

Don't Stop Believin' was only a minor hit in Australia, and failed to break Olivia's run of chart failures in the UK.

16 ~ EVERY FACE TELLS A STORY

Australia: Interfusion K6599 (1977).
  B-side: *Love You Hold The Key*.

Every Face Tells A Story wasn't a hit in Australia.

UK: EMI EMI 2574 (1977).
  B-side: *Love You Hold The Key*.

Every Face Tells A Story wasn't a hit in the UK.

Canada
20.11.76: 97-90-67-66-62-**58-58-58**

South Africa
23.04.77: peaked at no.**5**, charted for 9 weeks

USA
6.11.76: 76-66-62-56-58-57-**55**-78-78

Every Face Tells A Story was originally written as *Every Face Tells A Story (It Never Tells A Lie)* by Michael Allison and Peter Still, with religious lyrics, for Cliff Ricard, who recorded it for his 1977 album, *EVERY FACE TELLS A STORY*.

Don Black completely re-wrote the lyrics, turning *Every Face Tells A Story* into a non-religious song. This is the version Olivia recorded for her 1976 album, *DON'T STOP BELIEVIN'*.

Every Face Tells A Story owes its Top 40 status to its popularity in South Africa, where it achieved no.5. It was much less successful in other countries, and peaked outside the Top 40 in Canada and the USA. In the USA, by stalling at no.55, the single brought to an end Olivia's run of nine consecutive Top 40 singles.

Every Face Tells A Story fared even less well in Australia and the UK, where it failed to enter the charts at all.

17 ~ SAM

Australia: Interfusion K-6674 (1977).
  B-side: *I'll Bet You A Kangaroo*.

28.03.77: peaked at no.**56**, charted for 39 weeks

UK: EMI 2626 (1977).
  B-side: *Changes*.

11.06.77: 33-23-12-9-**6**-8-8-13-18-26-34

Canada
5.02.77: 99-92-76-66-63-54-44-33-**26-26**-28-36-40-42-48

Ireland
6.07.77: 15-9-**1-1**-2-4-14-15

Japan
5.05.77: peaked at no.**57**, charted for 9 week

New Zealand
24.04.77: **16**-x-26-36-37-34-x-32

USA
29.01.77: 72-61-50-40-36-32-26-24-22-**20-20**-35-95

Sam was written by Don Black, John Farrar and Hank Marvin of The Shadows, and featured on Olivia's 1976 album, *DON'T STOP BELIEVIN'*.

Released as the third single from the album in early 1977, *Sam* enjoyed far greater success than the first two singles. It gave Olivia her first no.1 in Ireland, topping the chart for two weeks, and finally returned her to the singles chart in the UK, where it achieved a very respectable no.6.

Sam wasn't quite so successful in other countries, peaking at no. 16 in New Zealand, no.20 in the USA and no.26 in Canada, and charting outside the Top 50 in Australia and Japan. In Australia, despite only achieving no.56, *Sam* did enjoy an impressive 39 weeks on the chart.

18 ~ YOU'RE THE ONE THAT I WANT

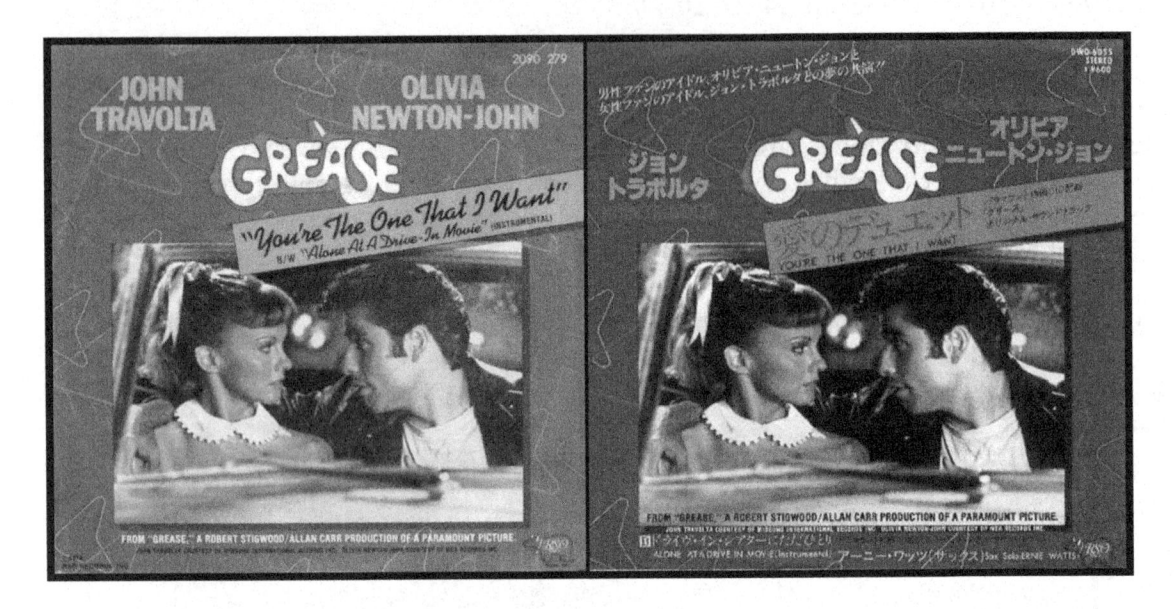

Australia: RSO 2090 279 (1978).
  B-side: *Alone At A Drive-In Movie (Instrumental)*.

29.05.78: peaked at no.**1** (9 weeks), charted for 32 weeks

UK: RSO 006 (1978); Polydor 044133-2 (1998).
  1978 B-side: *Alone At A Drive-In Movie (Instrumental)*.
  1998 B-side: *The Grease Megamix / You're The One That I Want (Video)*

20.05.78: 52-23-6-2-**1**-**1**-**1**-**1**-**1**-**1**-**1**-2-2-5-7-12-18-30-33-53-61-60-61-68
25.07.98: 4-16-24-31-52-62-61-71-69-84-x-x-x-94

Austria
15.07.78: 14-3-**2**-3-4-8-23 (monthly)
26.07.98: 32-39-33-31-32-30-34-37-26-40-39-39 (Remix)

Canada
15.04.78: 80-46-30-23-14-6-4-**2**-**2**-**2**-**2**-**2**-6-18-23-32-48-51-61-54-69-71-81

Germany
12.06.78: 28-18-10-8-2-2-2-2-2-**1**-2-**1**-**1**-2-**1**-**1**-**1**-2-2-4-9-12-11-13-14-18-23-23-23-29-23-
  36-46-41-x-50

Ireland
9.06.78: 5-2-4-**1-1-1-1-1-1-1-1**-2-1-5-13-10-15-18-19-29-27
16.07.98: 25-21-19-15-20-24-36

Japan
21.06.78: peaked at no.**25**, charted for 33 weeks

Netherlands
10.06.78: 40-5-2-2-**1-1-1-1-1-1-1-1**-2-2-2-2-6-9-9-13-19-23-28-41
27.06.98: 100-93-80-65-65-62-67-72-78-85 (Remix)

New Zealand
28.05.78: 29-3-**1-1-1-1**-2-2-2-2-3-3-4-7-9-12-12-14-16-18-12-21-31-28-28-35-38

Norway
22.07.78: 5-5-4-2-**1-1-1-1-1-1-1-1-1-1-1-1-1-1-1-1-1-1**-2-4-4-4-4-5-9-10

South Africa
22.07.78: peaked at no.**2**, charted for 18 weeks

Spain
9.10.78: peaked at no.**1** (8 weeks), charted for 25 weeks

Sweden
14.07.78: 13-8-3-2-4-2-2-**1-1-1-1-1-1**-2-4-11-15 (bi-weekly)

Switzerland
8.07.78: 14-13-8-6-6-5-3-3-**1-1-1-1-1-1-1**-2-2-3-4-5-10-14
26.07.98: 42-34 (Remix)

USA
1.04.78: 65-30-19-11-9-7-6-4-3-2-**1**-2-4-11-14-33-31-44-42-42-60-60-83-83

You're The One That I Want was written by John Farrar, and was recorded as a duet by Olivia with John Travolta, for the 1978 film *Grease*, in which they starred as Sandy Olsson and Danny Zuko, respectively.

In most countries, the duet was released as a single before *Grease* premiered, and was hugely successful. It hit no.1 in numerous countries, and enjoyed lengthy stints at the top of the chart in many: 18 weeks in Norway, 12 weeks in Sweden, nine weeks in Australia, Ireland and the UK, eight weeks in the Netherlands and Spain, seven weeks in Switzerland, six weeks in Germany and four weeks in New Zealand.

In the USA, *You're The One That I Want* spent a solitary week atop Billboard's Hot 100, and the single charted at no.2 in Austria, Canada and South Africa, and no.25 in Japan.

British comedians Arthur Mulland and Hylda Baker recorded a cover of *You're The One That I Want*, that is best remembered for their truly awful performance of the song on *Top Of the Pops* – despite which, the single charted at no.22 in the UK.

You're The One That I Want was reissued in many countries in 1998, to mark the 20th anniversary of *Grease*. This saw the single re-entering the charts in the UK and Ireland, where it peaked at no.4 and no.15, respectively.

In other countries, a dance remix – the Martian Remix – was released, and this version charted at no.26 in Austria and no.34 in Switzerland.

With global sales of around 15 million, *You're The One That I Want* is one of the best-selling singles of all-time. It has sold over two million copies in the UK alone, where it is the no.5 best-selling single of all-time.

John Travolta
Olivia Newton-John
GREASE is the word
A ROBERT STIGWOOD/ALLAN CARR PRODUCTION
JOHN TRAVOLTA OLIVIA NEWTON-JOHN "GREASE"
and STOCKARD CHANNING as Rizzo with special guest appearances by EVE ARDEN, FRANKIE AVALON
JOAN BLONDELL, EDD BYRNES, SID CAESAR, ALICE GHOSTLEY, DODY GOODMAN, SHA-NA-NA
BRONTE WOODARD ALLAN CARR JIM JACOBS WARREN CASEY
KENNETH WAISSMAN and MAXINE FOX PATRICIA BIRCH
ROBERT STIGWOOD and ALLAN CARR RANDAL KLEISER

19 ~ HOPELESSLY DEVOTED TO YOU

Australia: RSO 2090 309 (1978).
B-side: *Love Is A Many Splendoured Thing (Instrumental)*.

14.08.78: peaked at no.**2**, charted for 21 weeks

UK: RSO 017 (1978).
B-side: *Love Is A Many Splendoured Thing (Instrumental)*.

4.11.78: 24-4-**2**-**2**-3-10-26-45-45-57-59

Canada
29.07.78: 90-46-21-18-14-10-6-5-5-**1**-**1**-4-10-14-14-14-17-41-91

Ireland
1.09.78: 25-23-x-23-x-x-28-18-16-14-8-2-**1**-4-7-11-20-29-30

Netherlands
16.09.78: 22-11-2-**1**-**1**-**1**-**1**-2-3-7-14-18-23-26-34-47

New Zealand
10.09.78: 14-7-7-**6**-7-15-11-10-9-17-26-33-33

USA
8.07.78: 68-58-35-26-18-11-11-7-5-4-4-**3-3**-7-10-19-34-79-100

Like *You're The One That I Want*, *Hopelessly Devoted To You* was written by John Farrar, for the 1978 film, *Grease* – however, midway through the shooting of the film, the solo song Olivia was contracted to record for the film still hadn't been written, and when Farrar submitted *Hopelessly Devoted To You*, the film's production team were initially reluctant to accept it.

Hopelessly Devoted To You was released as the follow-up to *You're The One That I Want* in some countries, but was preceded by *Summer Nights* in others. The single was never going to match the success of *You're The One That I Want*, but it did give Olivia one of her biggest solo hits, going to no.1 in Canada, Ireland and the Netherlands, no.2 in Australia and the UK, no.3 in the USA and no.6 in New Zealand.

In the USA, *Hopelessly Devoted To You* was nominated for an Academy Award, for Best Original Song, but the Oscar went to *Last Dance*, which Donna Summer performed in *Thank God It's Friday*. Olivia also picked up another Grammy nomination, for Best Pop Vocal Performance, Female, but this time she lost out to Anne Murray's *You Needed Me*.

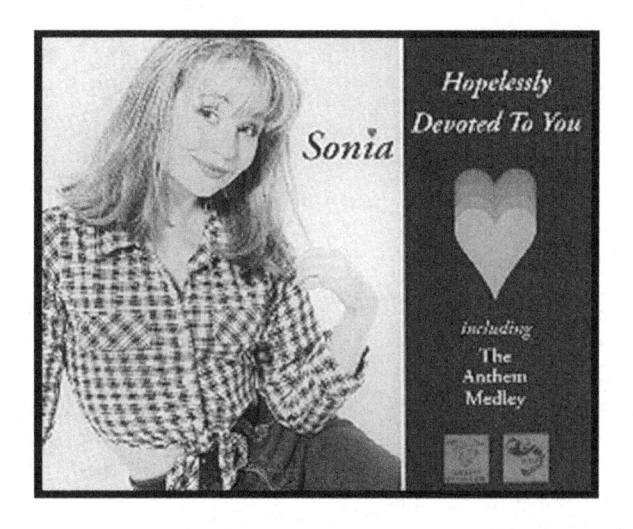

In 1994, when she took over the role of Sandy from Debbie Gibson in the West End production of *Grease*, Sonia released a cover of *Hopelessly Devoted To You* in the UK, but only a minor no.61 hit resulted.

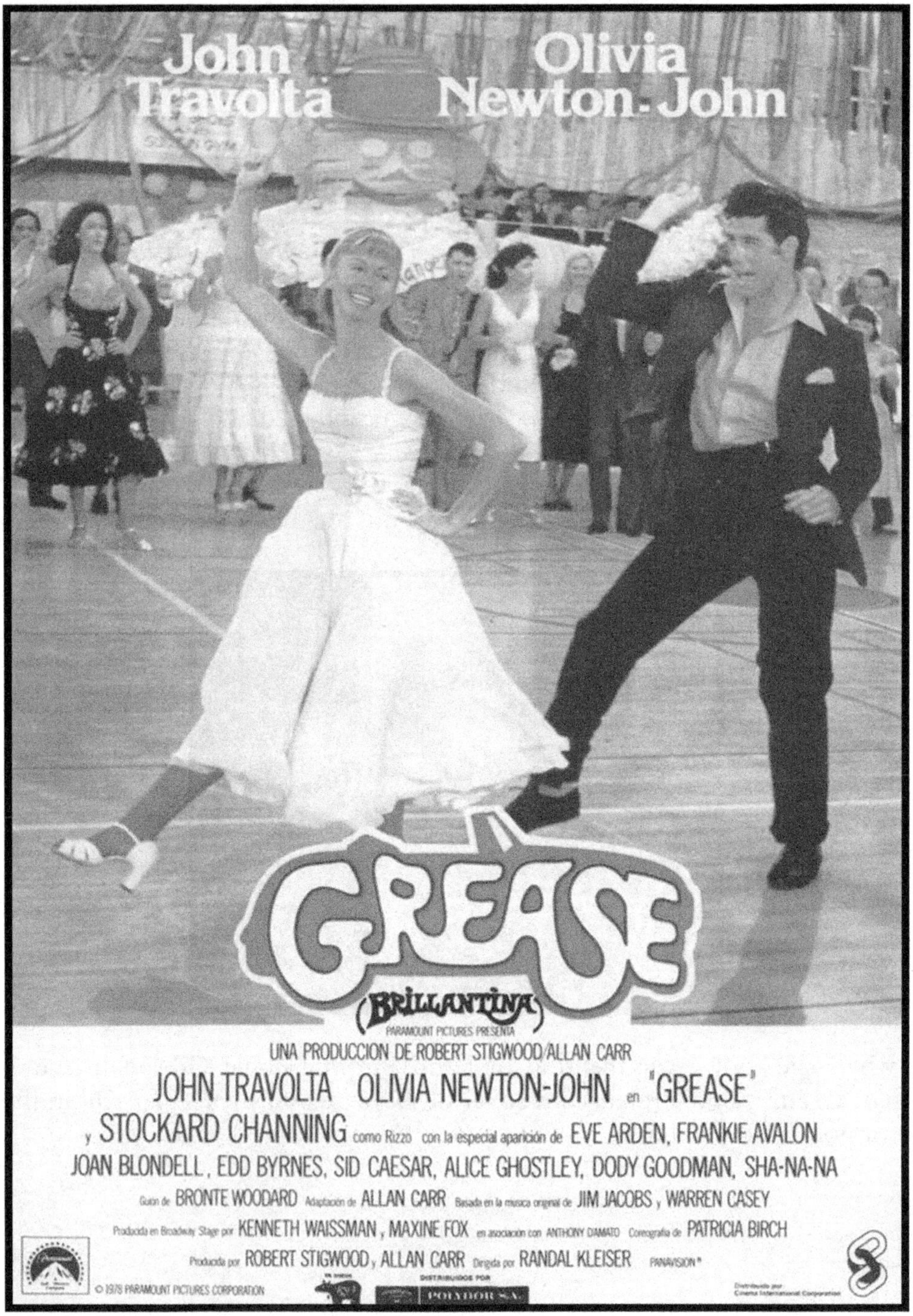
John Travolta
Olivia Newton-John
GREASE
BRILLANTINA
PARAMOUNT PICTURES PRESENTA
UNA PRODUCCION DE ROBERT STIGWOOD/ALLAN CARR
JOHN TRAVOLTA OLIVIA NEWTON-JOHN en "GREASE"
y STOCKARD CHANNING como Rizzo con la especial aparición de EVE ARDEN, FRANKIE AVALON
JOAN BLONDELL, EDD BYRNES, SID CAESAR, ALICE GHOSTLEY, DODY GOODMAN, SHA-NA-NA
Guion de BRONTE WOODARD Adaptación de ALLAN CARR Basada en la musica original de JIM JACOBS y WARREN CASEY
Producida en Broadway Stage por KENNETH WAISSMAN, MAXINE FOX en asociación con ANTHONY D'AMATO Coreografía de PATRICIA BIRCH
Producida por ROBERT STIGWOOD y ALLAN CARR Dirigida por RANDAL KLEISER PANAVISION®
© 1978 PARAMOUNT PICTURES CORPORATION
DISTRIBUIDOS POR
POLYDOR S.A.
Distribuida por
Cinema International Corporation

20 ~ SUMMER NIGHTS

Australia: RSO 2090 316 (1978).
  B-side: *Rock'n'Roll Party Queen*.

9.10.78: peaked at no.**6**, charted for 16 weeks

UK: RSO 018 (1978).
  B-side: *Rock'n'Roll Party Queen*.

16.09.78: 56-11-**1**-**1**-**1**-**1**-**1**-**1**-**1**-3-7-15-30-44-53-53-52-71-71

Austria
15.11.78: 5-**1**-10 (monthly)

Canada
19.08.78: 89-59-35-22-11-9-?-**3**-**3**-**3**-15-15-15-19-52-79

Germany
8.10.78: 32-13-9-6-8-**4**-8-10-13-20-16-21-22-19-28-31-30-45

Ireland
29.09.78: 3-2-**1**-**1**-**1**-4-4-3-5-7-9-19-28-x-22-20

Japan
21.10.78: peaked at no.**46**, charted for 8 weeks

New Zealand
22.10.78: **3**-4-4-7-13-16-24-27

Netherlands
30.09.78: 8-3-2-2-2-**1**-4-6-11-21-28-35-48

Norway
4.11.78: 10-3-3-**2-2-2-2**-4-6-7-7-7-7-9

South Africa
28.10.78: peaked at no.**10**, charted for 7 weeks

Spain
12.02.79: peaked at no.**18**, charted for 3 weeks

Sweden
20.10.78: 13-5-**3-3-3**-7-9-14-16-17 (bi-weekly)

Switzerland
4.11.78: 13-11-8-9-**7**-10-13-13-13-14

USA
5.08.78: 66-46-29-21-15-8-7-6-**5-5**-9-10-12-37-66-97

Summer Nights was written by Jim Jacobs and Warren Casey, for the 1971 stage musical, *Grease* – it also featured in the original Broadway production, which premiered on 7th June 1972 at the Broadhurst Theater.

For the 1978 film version of *Grease*, Olivia recorded *Summer Nights* with co-star John Travolta, but unlike *You're The One That I Want* the recording also featured other members of the cast.

Released as a single, *Summer Nights* – like *You're The One That I Want* – was hugely successful. In the UK, the single went to no.1 for seven straight weeks, meaning Olivia and John's two duets had topped the charts for an impressive 16 weeks combined. The single went on to sell 1.6 million copies in the UK alone.

Summer Nights hit no.1 in Austria, Ireland and the Netherlands as well, and charted at no.2 in Norway, no.3 in Canada, New Zealand and Sweden, no.4 in Germany, no.5 in the USA, no.6 in Australia, no.7 in Switzerland, no.10 in South Africa and no.18 in Spain.

In 1991, *Summer Nights* and *You're The One That I Want*, along with John Travolta's *Greased Lightnin'*, were released as *The Grease Megamix*, and became a hit all over again.

Seven years later, to celebrate the 20th anniversary of the film, *You're The One That I Want* and *Summer Nights* were remixed – the 'Martian Remixes' – and re-released. This time, however, while *You're The One That I Want* was a hit again in several countries, *Summer Nights* proved less popular and failed to chart.

In 2010, *Summer Nights* was ranked at no.9 in Billboard magazine's list of the 'Best Summer Songs Of All Time'.

21 ~ A LITTLE MORE LOVE

Australia: Interfusion K7289 (1978).
  B-side: *Borrowed Time*.

20.11.78: peaked at no.**9**, charted for 20 weeks

UK: EMI 2879 (1978).
  B-side: *Borrowed Time*.

16.12.78: 54-32-32-21-12-5-**4**-6-10-16-42-67

Canada
9.12.78: 84-57-48-32-32-21-15-13-10-7-4-**2-2-2**-4-5-6-14-18-30-41

Germany
12.02.79: 48-x-49-**34**-35-43-45

Ireland
8.12.78: 15-12-9-11-10-9-**4**-5-**4**-6-10-28

Netherlands
9.12.78: 32-24-12-9-7-6-5-**4**-7-21-22-49-41

New Zealand
21.01.79: 21-17-**7**-8-9-9-10-11-14-15-20-23-37

Norway
13.01.79: 10-**6**-7-**6**-7-8-9-x-x-10

Sweden
1.12.78: **12-12**-13-20-15-15 (bi-weekly)

USA
25.11.78: 68-52-35-26-19-19-13-11-8-6-4-4-**3-3**-5-6-9-10-20-55

Following the enormous success of *Grease* and the singles lifted from it, Olivia's next solo project *TOTALLY HOT* was eagerly anticipated.

The album was preceded by a single written and produced by John Farrar, *A Little More Love*, which was well received and gave Olivia one of her biggest solo hits around the world.

A Little More Love narrowly failed to make no.1 in Canada, where it spent three weeks in the runner-up spot, and elsewhere it achieved no.3 in the USA, no.4 in Ireland, the Netherlands and the UK, no.6 in Norway, no.7 in New Zealand, no.9 in Australia, no.12 in Sweden and no.34 in Germany.

Borrowed Time, the B-side of *A Little More Love* in most countries, also featured on the album *TOTALLY HOT*, and was composed by Olivia.

22 ~ DEEPER THAN THE NIGHT

Australia: Interfusion K7445 (1979).
  B-side: *Please Don't Keep Me Waiting*.

16.07.79: peaked at no.**74**, charted for 6 weeks

UK: EMI 2954 (1979).
  B-side: *Please Don't Keep Me Waiting*.

30.06.79: 65-**64**-70

Canada
28.04.79: 89-64-55-42-30-22-**18**-19-26-36-47-78

USA
14.04.79: 79-68-45-35-25-18-16-12-**11**-29-37-49-90

Deeper Than The Night was written by Tom Snow and Johnny Vastano, and was chosen as the second single from Olivia's album, *TOTALLY HOT*.
  The single was only a minor hit in Australia and the UK, but was more successful in North America, where it charted at no.11 in the USA and no.18 in Canada.
  In the USA, MCA released a promotional 7" picture disc, which was mastered at the wrong speed: the song sounded speeded-up if played at 45rpm, and too slow if played at

33rpm. The promo came with a thank you card from Olivia's record company, and was also issued as a double-pack, which also included a standard black vinyl 7" single.

One further single was released from *TOTALLY HOT*, the album's title cut b/w *Dancin' 'Round And 'Round*, but neither achieved Top 40 status anywhere.

23 ~ I CAN'T HELP IT

Australia: RSO K-7851 (1980).
  B-side: *Someone I Ain't*.

9.06.80: peaked at no.**62**, charted for 8 weeks

UK: RSO 59 (1980).
  B-side: *Someone I Ain't*.

I Can't Help It wasn't a hit in the UK.

Canada
12.04.80: 96-88-80-70-61-52-52-46-35-**32**-38-38-52-57-66-70-72

Spain
30.06.80: peaked at no.**23**, charted for 7 weeks

USA
29.03.80: 63-50-43-32-21-17-14-13-**12-12**-24-60-93

I Can't Help It was written by Barry Gibb of the Bee Gees, and was recorded as a duet with Olivia by Barry's younger brother, Andy.

Released as a single, the duet charted at no.12 in the USA, no. 23 in Spain and no.32 in Canada, but was only a minor hit in Australia and missed the chart in most countries, including the UK.

I Can't Help It featured on two albums, Andy Gibb's *AFTER DARK* and the charity compilation *THE MUSIC FOR UNICEF CONCERT: A GIFT OF SONG*, which also included contributions from Andy Gibb solo, ABBA, the Bee Gees, John Denver, Earth, Wind & Fire, Kris Kristofferson & Rita Coolidge, Rod Stewart and Donna Summer.

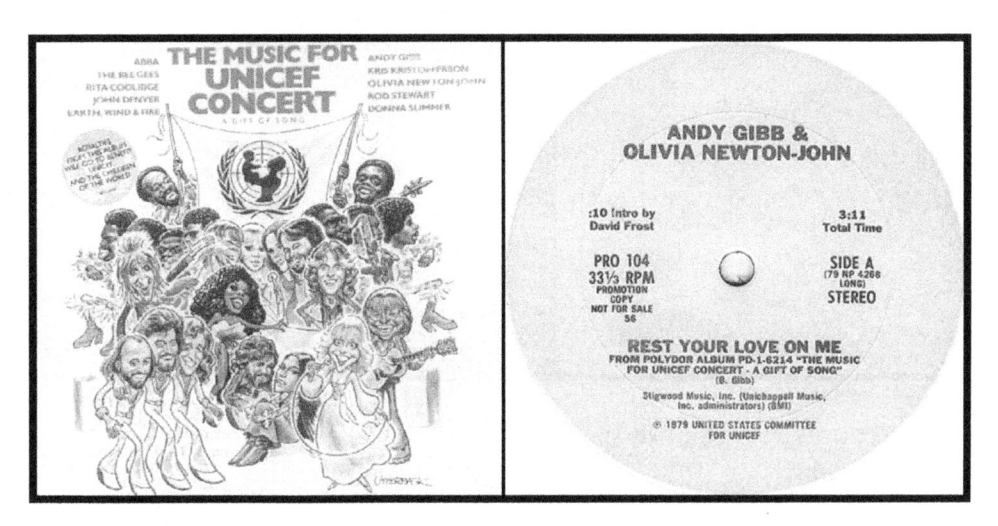

Andy Gibb's *AFTER DARK* album featured a second duet with Olivia, *Rest Your Love On Me*, which was also written by Andy's brother, Barry. The track was released as a promotional single in several countries, but it wasn't a hit anywhere.

24 ~ MAGIC

Australia: Jet Records JS 018 (1980).
   B-side: *Fool Country.*

7.07.80: peaked at no.**4**, charted for 18 weeks
5.06.11: 79   (Remix)

UK: Jet Records JET 196 (1980).
   B-side: *Whenever You're Away From Me.*

23.08.80: 56-**32**-34-34-60-51-73

Austria
15.11.80: **20**   (bi-weekly)

Canada
7.06.80: 81-73-58-53-45-24-13-9-9-5-2-2-2-**1**-**1**-2-6-7-20-21-27

Germany
27.10.80: 42-51-**36**-46-46-48-53-55-65-68

Japan
1.08.80: peaked at no.**43**, charted for 15 weeks

Netherlands
27.09.80: **13-13**-19-24-32-33

New Zealand
27.07.80: 35-29-12-7-6-**4-4-4**-8-11-11-16-18-33-42-45

South Africa
27.09.80: peaked at no.**5**, charted for 9 weeks

USA
24.05.80: 74-64-50-36-24-16-14-8-7-2-**1-1-1-1**-3-6-13-27-27-65-71-83-97

Following the success of *Grease*, Olivia was inundated with film scripts, and the one she chose was *Xanadu*, which was billed as 'A Fantasy. A Musical. A Place Where Dreams Come True.'

Xanadu was written by Richard Christian Danus and Marc Reid Rubel, and directed by Robert Greenwald. The accompanying soundtrack featured music by Olivia and the Electric Light Orchestra, and two lead singles were released: *Magic* by Olivia and *I'm Alive* by the Electric Light Orchestra.

Magic was written and produced by John Farrar, and gave Olivia her biggest hit to date in the USA, where it spent four weeks at no.1, The single also went to no.1 in Canada, and achieved no.4 in Australia and New Zealand, no.5 in South Africa, no.13 in the Netherlands, no.20 in Austria, no.32 in the UK, no.36 in Germany and no.43 in Japan.

In May 2011, two Australians – DJ Dan Murphy and Steve Peach – created a dance version of *Magic*. Olivia recorded new vocals for the Peachy & Murphy Remix, and the project was sponsored by a humanitarian group, WACCI, which was credited alongside Olivia on the recording.

The Peachy & Murphy Remix premiered on the Australian TV show, *Dancing With The Stars*, on 22nd May 2011, and was released exclusively on iTunes in Australia on the same day. A minor hit, all proceeds from the remix went to Olivia's cancer charity, The Olivia Newton-John Cancer and Wellness Centre.

Magic was completely reworked as an electronic dance track in 2015 by producer/remixer Dave Audé, and re-titled *You Have To Believe*.

Olivia's daughter Chloe Lattanzi and Vasiliki 'Vassy' Karagiorgos re-wrote the lyrics, and Olivia and Chloe recorded with track with Dave Audé.

'It was actually Chloe's idea to rework *Magic* and I was thrilled,' said Olivia, 'as she is not only a great singer but a talented writer. It was a great collaboration across the board. And, a fun fact is that I met Chloe's dad on the set of *Xanadu*, so, without that film, Chloe wouldn't be here. She was the real 'magic' that came out of that film!'

Although not a hit on any mainstream charts, *You Have To Believe* did go all the way to no.1 on Billboard's Hot Dance Club Songs chart – the first time ever, for a mother-daughter duo.

XANADU

Das Film-Musical 1980
mit Olivia Newton-John,
Electric Light Orchestra,
Michael Beck, Gene Kelly,
The Tubes, Cliff Richard u. v. m.

4 Hit-Singles aus dem orig. Soundtrack

Orig. Soundtrack Album

Übrigens: Ihr findet die z. Zt. berühmteste Pop-Gruppe nicht nur auf dem Orig. Soundtrack-Album sondern auch auf den beiden Hit-LP's.

E.L.O. Greatest Hits

E.L.O. Discovery

CBS
The Family of Music

Jet

25 ~ DON'T CRY FOR ME ARGENTINA

Australia: Interfusion K7852 (1978).
  B-side: *Gimme Some Lovin'*

16.06.80: peaked at no.**32**, charted for 14 weeks

Inspired by the life of the Argentinian leader Eva Perón, *Don't Cry For Me Argentina* was written by Tim Rice and Andrew Lloyd Webber, originally for their 1976 concept album, *EVITA*. The song was recorded by Julie Covington, and she took the single to no.1 in several countries, including Australia, Ireland, the Netherlands, New Zealand and the UK.

Olivia recorded *Don't Cry For Me Argentina* for her 1977 album, *MAKING A GOOD THING BETTER*. Her version was released as a single in Australia in 1978 and, although not a hit at the time, the single did belatedly achieve Top 40 status two years later, peaking at no.32.

EVITA premiered as a musical in 1978, and was made into a film in 1996, with Madonna in the starring role. Her recording of *Don't Cry For Me Argentina* was released as a single, and achieved Top 10 status in numerous countries.

Don't Cry For Me Argentina has been covered many times over the years, including versions by Shirley Bassey, Carpenters, Sinéad O'Connor and Donna Summer.

26 ~ XANADU

Australia: Jet Records JS 017 (1980).
  B-side: *Whenever You're Away From Me*.

18.08.80: peaked at no.**2**, charted for 17 weeks

UK: Jet Records JET 185 (1980).
  B-side: *Fool Country*.

21.06.80: 39-14-3-**1**-**1**-2-4-13-20-35-47

Austria
15.08.80: 2-2-**1**-**1**-4-4-8-12-16 (bi-weekly)

Canada
6.09.80: 82-66-51-36-14-**9**-**9**-**9**-15-34

Germany
14.07.80: 30-11-4-3-2-2-2-2-**1**-**1**-3-5-6-7-6-6-8-10-15-15-19-23-23-33-34-39-44-54-66

Ireland
5.07.80: 13-**1**-**1**-**1**-9 (bi-weekly)

Japan
21.08.80: peaked at no.**22**, charted for 27 weeks

Netherlands
28.06.80: 48-8-3-**1**-**1**-**1**-**1**-**1**-2-2-4-5-10-24-38-42-49

New Zealand
21.09.80: 29-26-**8**-11-13-23-32-35-29

Norway
28.06.80: 6-4-2-**1**-**1**-**1**-**1**-**1**-2-2-**1**-3-4-6

South Africa
20.12.80: **20**

Spain
20.10.80: peaked at no.**1** (6 weeks), charted for 24 weeks

Sweden
11.07.80: 10-8-6-6-4-5-**3**-**3**-**3**-6-10-x-10 (bi-weekly)

Switzerland
27.07.80: 14-9-3-**2**-**2**-**2**-**2**-**2**-3-5-6-8-10-13

USA
9.08.80: 79-63-43-31-26-17-12-11-10-**8**-**8**-17-27-51-58-73-94

Magic and the Electric Light Orchestra's single *I'm Alive* were followed by the film's and soundtrack's title cut, *Xanadu*, which was written and produced by the Electric Light Orchestra's Jeff Lynne. Olivia sang lead vocals on the recording, with Lynne on background vocals.

Xanadu was less successful than *Magic* in North America, but far more successful in Europe, where it hit no.1 in Austria, Germany, Ireland, the Netherlands, Norway, Spain and the UK. In the UK, *Xanadu* was the Electric Light Orchestra's only chart topper, and Olivia's third, following her collaborations with John Travolta, *You're The One That I Want* and *Summer Nights*.

Elsewhere, *Xanadu* charted at no.2 in Australia and Switzerland, no.3 in Sweden, no.8 in New Zealand and the USA, no.9 in Canada, no.20 in South Africa and no.22 in Japan.

In 2000, Jeff Lynne recorded a solo version of *Xanadu*, for inclusion on the Electric Light Orchestra's compilation *ALL OVER THE WORLD* and box-set *FLASHBACK*.

27 ~ SUDDENLY

Australia: Jet Records JS 019 (1980).
 B-side: *You Made Me Love You.*

27.10.80: peaked at no.**37**, charted for 12 weeks

UK: Jet Records JET 7002 (1980).
 B-side: *You Made Me Love You.*

25.10.80: 43-25-**15**-17-20-27-53

Canada
8.11.80: 65-**60**

Ireland
2.11.80: 28-9-8-**6**-15-21

New Zealand
18.01.81: 41-43-50-37-41-**30**-40

USA
25.10.80: 79-69-58-48-39-35-30-28-25-23-23-21-**20**-24-38-47-56-73-98

Suddenly was written and produced by John Farrar, and was recorded by Olivia as a duet with Cliff Richard, for the *XANADU* soundtrack – it was the third single to feature Olivia released as a single.

Although it wasn't as successful as *Magic* or *Xanadu*, *Suddenly* sold reasonably well, and was a Top 10 hit in Ireland, where it rose to no.6. The single charted at no.15 in the UK, no.20 in the USA, no.30 in New Zealand, no.37 in Australia and no.60 in Canada.

28 ~ PHYSICAL

Australia: Interfusion K8480 (1981).
  B-side: *The Promise (The Dolphin Song)*.

26.10.81: peaked at no.**1** (5 weeks), charted for 28 weeks
6.06.10: 88 (with Glee Cast)

UK: EMI 5234 (1981).
  B-side: *The Promise (The Dolphin Song)*.

10.10.81: 57-45-40-29-18-11-**7**-8-11-19-35-36-36-33-58-62
22.05.10: 56 (with Glee Cast)

Austria
1.12.81: **7-7**-12-14 (bi-weekly)

Canada
24.10.81: 38-28-21-12-10-9-5-4-**1-1-1-1-1-1**-2-2-5-5-5-510-12-12-14-14-21-22-27-32

Germany
2.11.81: 13-9-9-9-7-7-**4**-5-6-12-9-10-13-15-15-24-28-47-53-51-69

Ireland
22.11.81: 13-6-**4**-11-29

Japan
21.10.81: peaked at no.**17**, charted for 25 weeks

Netherlands
17.10.81: 39-32-18-14-9-**6**-9-14-11-20-29-49-30-43

New Zealand
15.11.81: 23-3-2-**1-1**-2-2-2-2-2-**1**-5-12-10-14-28-33-39

South Africa
14.08.82: peaked at no.**11**, charted for 6 weeks

Spain
29.03.82: peaked at no.**8**, charted for 10 weeks

Sweden
6.11.81: 19-**15**-20-20 (bi-weekly)

Switzerland
8.11.81: 9-3-2-**1-1-1-1**-3-3-8-12-14

USA
3.10.81: 66-47-31-26-23-14-3-**1-1-1-1-1-1-1-1-1-1**-4-7-8-9-17-31-46-56-95
22.05.10: 89 (with Glee Cast)

Physical was written by Steve Kipner and Terry Shaddick – originally, they planned to offer the song to Rod Stewart.

Olivia, despite serious reservations, recorded *Physical* in January 1981. 'I knew it was a great song and a hit for somebody,' she acknowledged, 'but then I had a panic attack. I thought, this song is way too out there, it's too sexual, it's way too bold and too cheeky.'

Olivia went so far as to call her manager Roger Davies, to ask him to pull the single's release, but he told her it was too late: it had already been sent to radio.

Raunchy lyrics, filled with sexual innuendo, led to *Physical* being censored and banned by some radio stations. In South Africa, the single was censored as offensive, and the line 'There's nothing left to talk about unless it's horizontally' was omitted. Olivia promoted the single with an equally controversial, but humorous, video that featured her in a gym with several muscular, scantily-clad men.

Despite the controversy, *Physical* went on to give Olivia the biggest hit of her career in the USA, where it topped the Hot 100 for ten straight weeks and sold more than two million copies. The single also went to no.1 in Australia, Canada, New Zealand and Switzerland, and achieved no.4 in Germany and Ireland, no.6 in the Netherlands, no.7 in Austria and the UK, no.8 in Spain, no.11 in South Africa, no.15 in Sweden and no.17 in Japan.

Olivia picked up two Grammy nominations for *Physical*, losing out to Lena Horne's *LENA HORNE: THE LADY AND HER MUSIC* in the Best Pop Vocal Performance, Female category, but winning an award for Video Of The Year.

Physical ranked at no.1 in Billboard magazine's End of Decade 1980-89 Hot 100 chart, making it the most successful single of the 1980s in the USA.

In 2002, Olivia released a Bossa Nova version of *Physical* as a bonus track on her Australian duets album, *(2)*.

Olivia made a guest appearance on the 'Bad Reputation' episode of the popular TV show *Glee* in 2010, and sang *Physical* as a duet with Jane Lynch. The episode premiered on 4th May in the USA, and on 20th May in Australia. Digital sales saw the duet achieving no.56 in the UK, and the track was a minor hit in Australia and the USA.

29 ~ LANDSLIDE

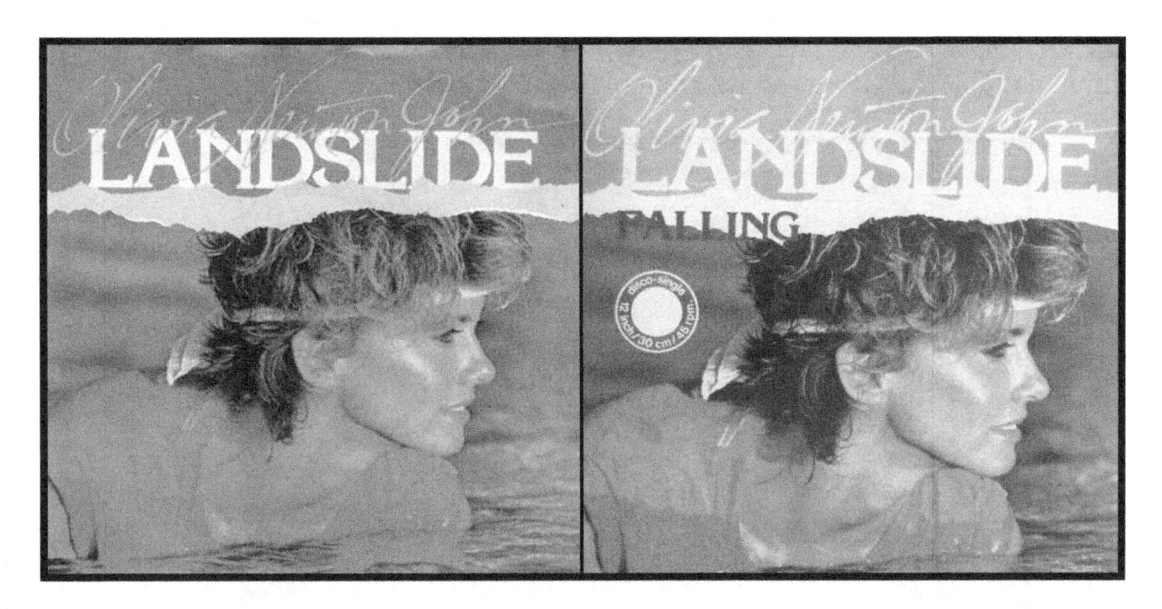

Australia: Interfusion K8757 (1981).
  B-side: *Recovery*.

Landslide wasn't a hit in Australia.

UK: EMI 5257 (1982).
  B-side: *Falling*.

16.01.82: 43-35-29-44-32-**18**-27-33-69

Ireland
7.02.82: **25**-30-29-27

Netherlands
30.01.82: **39**-43

USA
12.06.82: 82-72-58-**52-52**-60-76-98

Landslide was written and produced by John Farrar – it was the second single released from Olivia's album *PHYSICAL* in the UK, and the third in most other countries, where it followed *Make A Move On Me*.

Given the success of *Physical*, Olivia might have expected *Landslide* would be a bigger hit than it was. The single only achieved Top 40 status in three countries, peaking at no.18 in the UK, no.25 in Ireland and no.39 in the Netherlands. The single charted at a disappointing no.52 in the USA, and wasn't a hit in most countries, including Australia.

30 ~ MAKE A MOVE ON ME

Australia: Interfusion K8627 (1981).
  B-side: *Falling*.

15.02.82: peaked at no.**8**, charted for 15 weeks

UK: EMI 5291 (1981).
  B-side: *Stranger's Touch*.

17.04.82: 61-**43**-55

Canada
13.02.82: 43-38-28-18-11-9-6-**4**-7-10-8-9-10-16-25-31

Germany
8.02.82: **38**-58-46-52-57-56-63-68

Japan
21.02.82: peaked at no.**59**, charted for 12 weeks

Netherlands
17.04.82: **49**

New Zealand
25.04.82: 29-27-**22**-35-30-35-33

USA
13.02.82: 69-49-39-19-17-7-6-**5-5-5**-13-24-80-94

Released as the second single from Olivia's *PHYSICAL* album in most countries, *Make A Move On Me* was more successful than *Landslide* in many, the UK and Ireland being two exceptions.

Make A Move On Me Was written by John Farrar and Tom Snow, and produced by Farrar. The single achieved Top 10 status in three countries, rising to no.4 in Canada, no.5 in the USA and no.8 in Australia,

Elsewhere, *Make A Move On Me* charted at no.22 in New Zealand, no.38 in Germany, no.43 in the UK, no.49 in the Netherlands and no.59 in Japan.

31 ~ HEART ATTACK

Australia: Interfusion K8850 (1982).
  B-side: *Stranger's Touch*.

4.10.82: peaked at no.**22**, charted for 16 weeks

UK: EMI 5347 (1982).
  B-side: *Recovery*.

23.10.82: 70-**46**-56-63

Austria
15.11.82: 17-13-15-19-**7** (bi-weekly)

Canada
18.09.82: 44-38-25-17-10-3-**2**-**2**-4-7-11-12-17-21-38-38-41

Germany
15.11.82: **51**-62-74-68-x-75

Ireland
7.11.82: **30**

Japan
1.10.82: peaked at no.**71**, charted for 9 weeks

New Zealand
31.10.82: 29-25-16-13-**11**-13-14-19-19-19-19-19-42-46-35-48

Norway
25.09.82: 9-**5**-10-8

South Africa
27.11.82: peaked at no.**4**, charted for 12 weeks

USA
4.09.82: 67-58-51-39-13-11-9-6-6-**3-3-3-3**-16-16-24-46-46-59-89-100

Heart Attack was one of two new songs Olivia recorded for her 1982 compilation, *GREATEST HITS VOLUME 2*, which was released – with a slightly different sleeve design and a different track listing – as *OLIVIA'S GREATEST HITS* in the UK. The second new song, *Tied Up*, was also released as a single.

Written by Steve Kipner and Paul Bliss, *Heart Attack* was more successful than *Make A Move On Me*, and charted at no.2 in Canada, no.3 in the USA, no.4 in South Africa, no.5 in Norway, no.7 in Austria, no.11 in New Zealand, no.22 in Australia, no.30 in Ireland, no.46 in the UK and no.51 in Germany.

32 ~ TIED-UP

Australia: Interfusion K8948 (1982).
  B-side: *Silvery Rain*.

21.02.83: peaked at no.**54**, charted for 10 weeks

UK: EMI 5375 (1982).
  B-side: *Silvery Rain*.

Tied-Up wasn't a hit in the UK.

Canada
5.02.83: 48-**43-43**-44

USA
15.01.83: 76-64-52-45-41-**38-38-38**-60-89-98

Tied Up was the second new song Olivia recorded for her 1982 compilation, *GREATEST HITS VOLUME 2*, which was released as *OLIVIA'S GREATEST HITS* in the UK.
  Composed by John Farrar and Lee Ritenour, *Tied Up* fared less well than *Heart Attack*, and owes its Top 40 status to the no.38 placing it achieved in the USA. The single also charted at no.43 in Canada and no.54 in Australia, but failed to chart in most countries, including the UK.

33 ~ TWIST OF FATE

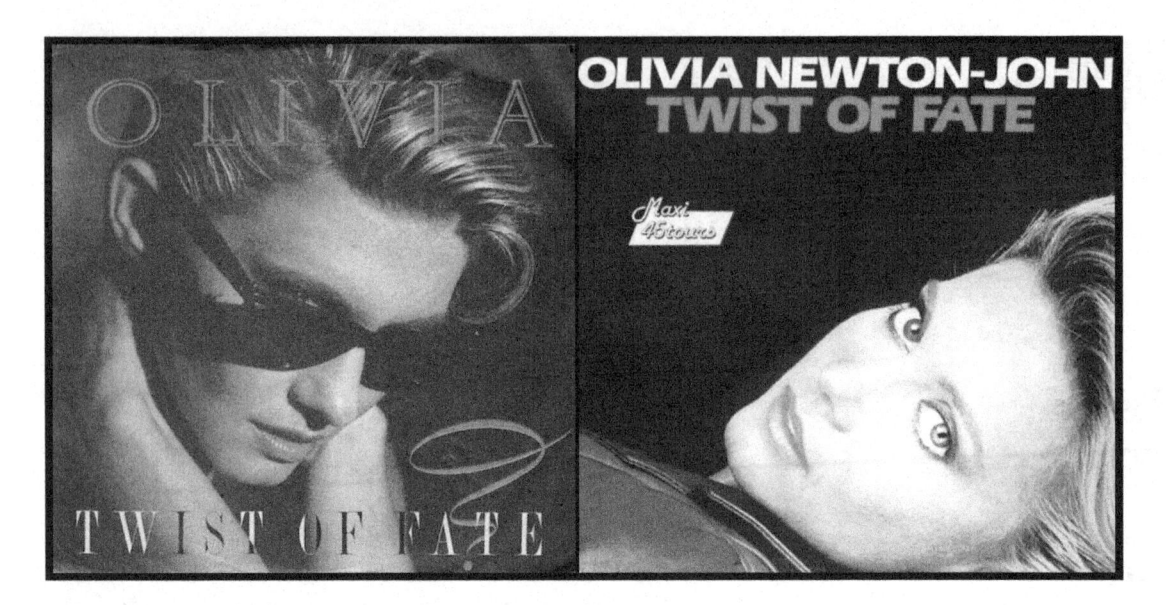

Australia: Interfusion K9279 (1983).
  B-side: *Coolin' Down*.

28.11.83: peaked at no.**4**, charted for 20 weeks

UK: EMI 5438 (1983).
  B-side: *Jolene*.

5.11.83: 98-73-**57**-80

Canada
5.11.83: 48-44-34-27-22-21-20-14-11-11-6-**5**-**5**-7-10-21-32

Japan
21.11.83: peaked at no.**73**, charted for 11 weeks

Netherlands
3.12.83: **42**-48-x-49

New Zealand
22.01.84: 30-34-**22**-25-30-30-42

South Africa
14.01.84: peaked at no.**5**, charted for 10 weeks

Switzerland
25.12.83: 27-30-22-29-**20**-30

USA
5.11.83: 49-38-32-21-16-12-9-8-8-**5**-**5**-7-9-17-30-48-59-94

Written by Steve Kipner and Peter Beckett, and produced by David Foster, *Twist Of Fate* is a song Olivia recorded for the soundtrack of the 1983 film, *Two Of A Kind*, which saw her reunited with her *Grease* co-star, John Travolta.

Twist Of Fate saw Olivia return to the Top 10 in several countries, as it charted at no.4 in Australia, and no.5 in Canada, South Africa and the USA. The single also achieved no.20 in Switzerland, no.22 in New Zealand, no.42 in the Netherlands and no.57 in the UK.

Olivia's promo video *for Twist Of Fate*, directed by Brian Grant and David Mallet, was nominated for a Grammy, for Best Music Video, Short Form, but the award went to David Bowie for *Jazzin' For Blue Jeans*.

34 ~ LIVIN' IN DESPERATE TIMES

Australia: Interfusion K9331 (1984).
  B-side: *Landslide*.

19.03.84: peaked at no.**81**, charted for 5 weeks

UK: Not Released.

Canada
10.03.84: 49-44-**43-43**

USA
11.02.84: 64-46-40-35-33-**31-31**-41-66-99

Livin' In Desperate Times was written by Barry Alfonso and Tom Snow, and produced by David Foster.

  Like *Twist Of Fate*, Olivia recorded *Livin' In Desperate Times* for the *TWO OF A KIND* soundtrack, but as a single it disappointed and owes its Top 40 status to the no.31 it achieved in the USA. The single peaked just outside the Top 40 in Canada and was a minor hit in Australia, but it didn't chart anywhere else.

35 ~ SOUL KISS

Australia: Interfusion K9835 (1985).
  B-side: *Electric*.

28.10.85: peaked at no.**20**, charted for 14 weeks

UK: Mercury MER 210 (1985).
  B-side: *Electric*.

8.02.86: **100**

Canada
12.10.85: ?-93-46-32-27-26-**21**-22-**21**-28-?-46-54-54-65-92

Netherlands
26.10.85: 44-42-**38**-46-40-47

USA
5.10.85: 63-54-44-34-30-24-21-**20**-22-34-52-78-96-96-98

Soul Kiss was written by Mark Goldenberg, and was the lead single and title cut from Olivia's 13th studio album.

Soul Kiss achieved Top 40 status in four countries, charting at no.20 in Australia and the USA, no.21 in Canada and no.38 in the Netherlands. In the UK, disappointingly, the single spent a solitary week at no.100.

Olivia's husband at the time, and the father of her daughter Chloe, Matt Lattanzi, appeared in the music video for *Soul Kiss*. This was one of five promos Olivia filmed for tracks from *SOUL KISS*, which were released as a home video, also titled *Soul Kiss*. The other four were *Toughen Up*, *Emotional Tangle*, *Culture Shock* and *The Right Moment*.

36 ~ THE BEST OF ME

Australia: Atlantic 7-89420 (1986).
 B-side: *Sajé*.

The Best Of Me wasn't a hit in Australia.

UK: Atlantic A 9420 (1986).
 B-side: *Sajé*.

The Best Of Me wasn't a hit in the UK.

Canada
31.05.86: 92-75-69-66-54-46-35-26-20-**17-17**-23-29-34-35-40-44-57-67

USA
14.06.86: 89-87-83-**80**-88-92-94-96

Olivia worked with David Foster on the *TWO OF A KIND* soundtrack, and recorded *The Best Of Me* as a duet with him for his self-titled 1986, mostly instrumental album.
 Foster co-wrote *The Best Of Me* with Jeremy Lubbock and Richard Marx, and it was the second single lifted from the album, following *Love Theme From St. Elmo's Fire*, which rose to no.15 on the Hot 100 in the USA. *The Best Of Me* was less successful, struggling to no.80 in the USA and missing out in most countries, but achieving a respectable no.17 in Canada.

37 ~ THE RUMOUR

Australia: Interfusion K-613 (1988).
  B-side: *Winter Angel*.

11.09.88: 40-44-37-44-**35**-48-47

UK: Mercury MER 272 (1988).
  B-side: *Winter Angel*.

24.09.88: **85**-99

Canada
27.08.88: 76-69-63-57-53-**50**

Germany
3.10.88: **36-36-36**-38-43-55-51-60-68-75

USA
20.08.88: 90-84-68-**62**-63-86

The Rumour was written by Elton John and Bernie Taupin, and was recorded by Olivia for her 1988 album with the same title. As well as co-writing the song, Elton John also played piano and sang backing vocals on the recording.

The Rumour was released as the lead single from the album, but despite Elton John's involvement it wasn't a major hit. The single peaked at no.35 in Australia, no.36 in Germany, no.50 in Canada, no.62 in the USA and a lowly no.85 in the UK.

38 ~ THE GREASE MEGAMIX

Australia: Polydor 879 419-7 (1990).
  B-side: *Alone At The Drive-In Movie (Instrumental)*.

12.05.91: 36-22-13-6-**1**-**1**-**1**-**1**-**1**-2-3-4-5-8-8-9-14-19-26-29-34-40-48-49

UK: Polydor PO 114 (1990).
  B-side: *Alone At The Drive-In Movie (Instrumental)*.

22.12.90: 14-5-5-**3**-4-10-23-31-50-68
10.07.93: 97-x-96

Austria
17.03.91: 28-30-29-27-30-**26**-29

Canada
16.12.96: 86-86-86-86-62-54-50-**49**-63-86

Germany
4.03.91: 87-x-**42**-50-50-67-63-75-94

Ireland
23.12.90: 25-7-**4**-7-9-24

Netherlands
2.02.91: 91-60-28-15-10-7-**3-3**-4-7-9-12-18-29-35-52-66-86

New Zealand
21.04.91: 16-9-**7**-9-14-16-20-x-30-x-34-27-30-30-40-45

Norway
16.02.91: 8-8-6-**5**-6

Spain
4.03.91: peaked at no.**1** (12 weeks), charted for 25 weeks

Sweden
24.04.91: **35**-x-40 (bi-weekly)

The Grease Megamix, which was created by Phil Harding and Ian Curnow, was released to celebrate the release of the film *Grease* on home video. The megamix featured three hits from the film: *You're The One That I Want*, John Travolta's *Greased Lightnin'* and *Summer Nights*.

The Grease Megamix gave Olivia her biggest hit for years, hitting no.1 in Australia and Spain – it topped the chart for an impressive 12 weeks in Spain. The megamix also achieved no.3 in the Netherlands and the UK, no.4 in Ireland, no.5 in Norway, no.7 in New Zealand, no.26 in Austria, no.35 in Sweden, no.42 in Germany and no.49 in Canada.

As it wasn't released commercially, Billboard's chart rules at the time meant *The Grease Megamix* was ineligible to enter the Hot 100 in the USA.

To celebrate the 20th anniversary of *Grease*, *The Grease Megamix* was one of the tracks featured on *Grease – The Remix EP*, released in 1998.

39 ~ GREASE – THE DREAM MIX

Australia: Not Released.

UK: Polydor PO 136 (7") / 879 795-2 (Maxi-CD) (1991).
 7" B-side: *We Go Together*.
 Maxi-CD: *Grease – The Dream Mix (7" Version) / (12" Version) / We Go Together /
  Grease – The Dream Mix (7" Original Groove)*.

23.03.91: **47**-64

Netherlands
20.04.91: 65-37-18-13-**11**-18-23-40-66

Grease – The Dream Mix, like *The Grease Megamix*, was created by Phil Harding and Ian Curnow. This time, the three hits from *Grease* featured on the megamix were Frankie Valli's *Grease*, John Travolta's *Sandy* and Olivia's *Hopelessly Devoted To You*.
  Grease – The Dream Mix couldn't match the success of *The Grease Megamix*, and owes its Top 40 status to sales in the Netherlands, where it charted at no.11. The single also achieved no.47 in the UK, but it wasn't a hit in most countries.

40 ~ NO MATTER WHAT YOU DO

Australia: Festival Records D11769 (1994).
 B-side: *Silent Ruin*.

2.10.94: 42-**35**-40-48

UK: Red Bullet ONJPCD1 (promo, 1995).

No Matter What You Do wasn't a hit in the UK.

Olivia wrote and recorded *No Matter What You Do* for her 1994 album, *GAIA – ONE WOMAN'S JOURNEY*, which was the first album she released since she was diagnosed with breast cancer in 1992. For the first time, Olivia wrote all the songs on the album, which she also co-produced with Colin Bayley and Murray Burns.

 On the album's sleeve notes, of *No Matter What You Do*, Olivia wrote: 'This song came to me on the car on the way to the studio, it was during a time when I was having a lot of problems and I sent this song to all the negative forces in my life.' Olivia added the date she wrote the song, December 1993.

 No Matter What You Do was the only single released from *GAIA – ONE WOMAN'S JOURNEY*, and it achieved Top 40 status courtesy of its no.35 placing in Australia.

41 ~ HAD TO BE

Australia: EMI 882593.2 (1995).
  B-side: *Had To Be (Instrumental) / Don't Move Away*.

Had To Be wasn't a hit in Australia.

UK: EMI 7243 8 82592 2 4 (CD1) / 7243 8 82593 2 3 (CD2) (1995).
  CD1 B-side: *Had To Be (Live)* / Interview With John Cavanagh (BBC Radio Scotland).
  CD2 B-side: *Had To Be (Instrumental) / Don't Move Away*.

9.12.95: **22**-43-56-54-100

Had To Be was written by John Farrar and Tim Rice, for the 1996 stage musical, *Heathcliff*. The musical, loosely based on Emily Brontë's novel *Wuthering Heights*, was written by Cliff Richard, who also played the title role. The musical opened at the National Indoor Arena, Birmingham, England, on 16th October 1996.

Olivia recorded *Had To Be* as a duet with Cliff Richard, for his 1995 album, *SONGS FROM HEATHCLIFF*. The duet was only released as a single in a few countries, including Australia, the Netherlands and the UK, and it only charted in the UK, where it made its debut at no.22, but rose no higher.

Two CD singles were released in the UK, the second of which featured another duet Olivia had recorded with Cliff Richard as a bonus track, *Don't Walk Away*. This was the first duet Cliff recorded with a female artist, and was originally released as the B-side of his 1971 single, *Sunny Honey Girl*.

Olivia often appeared as a guest on Cliff's TV show in the 1970s, which he mentioned on the hand written note he included with the second CD.

> We sang duets on my T.V. series – way back – and I always loved the blend. Olivia has become a really good friend of mine and a massive star around the world since those days – so when I rang her about singing "Cathy" on my album and she was free and sounded keen, I was thrilled!
>
> So here is our first single with a bonus track that infact was our first recording together – Hope you like them both.
>
> Best wishes
> Cliff

42 ~ GREASE – THE REMIX EP

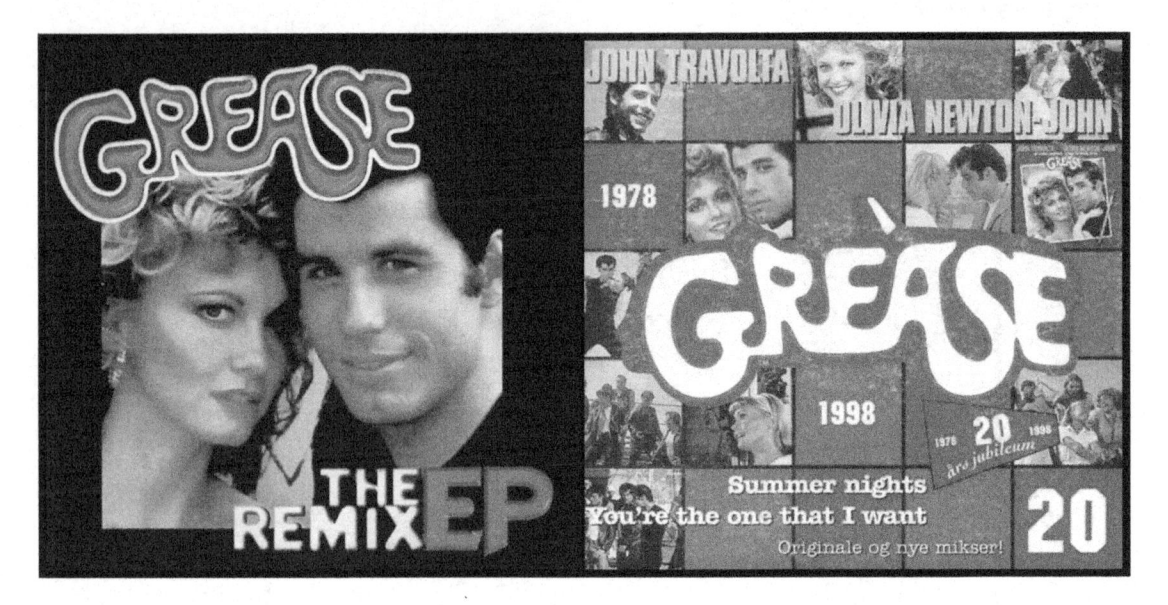

Australia: Polydor 567031-2 (1998).
  Tracks: *You're The One That I Want (Martian Mix) / Summer Nights (Martian Mix) / Grease Megamix (1991 PWL Version) / You're The One That I Want (Original Version) / Summer Nights (Original Version)*

24.05.98: 33-34-29-29-**27**-31-28-29-29-34-39-38-41

New Zealand
19.07.98: 46-**33**-38-45

Grease – The Remix EP was released in Australia to mark the 20th anniversary of *Grease*, and charted at no.27 in Australia and no.33 in New Zealand.
  CD singles, with slightly different titles and track listings, were also released in a few other countries, including France, Mexico, Norway and the USA, but none sold well enough to chart.

THE ALMOST TOP 40 SINGLES

Two of Olivia's singles have made the Top 50 in one or more countries, but failed to enter the Top 40 in any.

COMPASSIONATE MAN

This single, lifted from Olivia's 1976 album *DON'T STOP BELIEVIN'*, was only released in Japan, where it peaked at no.47 in early 1977.

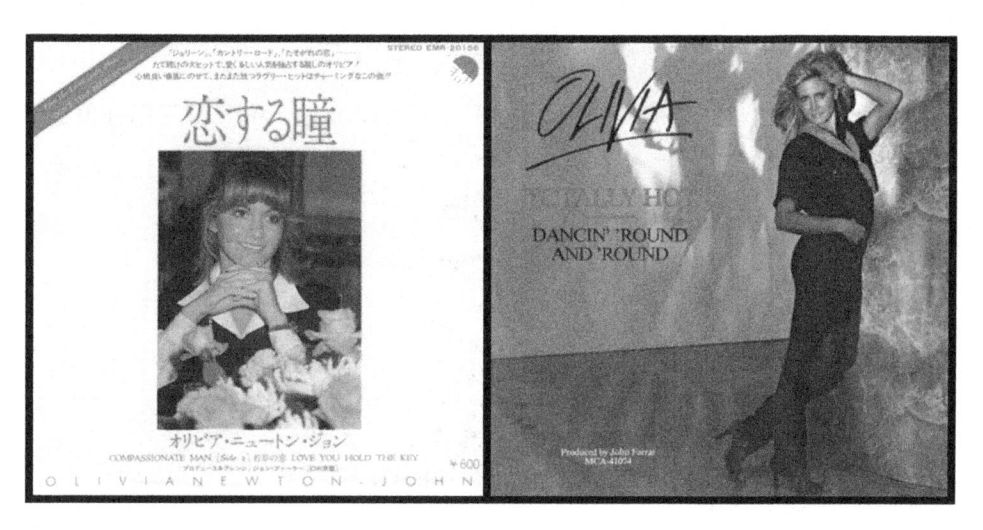

TOTALLY HOT

The title track of Olivia's 1978 album was released as the third single in most countries, but unlike the first two – *A Little More Love* and *Deeper Than The Night* – it failed to achieve Top 40 status anywhere. The closest it came was no.46 in the Netherlands, and it also charted at no.52 in the UK, but in most countries it failed to chart.

OLIVIA'S TOP 25 SINGLES

In this Top 40, each of Olivia's singles has been scored according to the following points system.

Points are given according to the peak position reached on the singles chart in each of the countries featured in this book:

    No.1:   100 points for the first week at no.1, plus 10 points for each additional week at no.1.

    No.2:   90 points for the first week at no.2, plus 5 points for each additional week at no.2.

No.3:	85 points.
No.4-6:	80 points.
No.7-10:	75 points.
No.11-15:	70 points.
No.16-20:	65 points.
No.21-30:	60 points.
No.31-40:	50 points.
No.41-50:	40 points.
No.51-60:	30 points.
No.61-70:	20 points.
No.71-80:	10 points.
No.81-100:	5 points.

Total weeks charted in each country are added, to give the final points score.

Reissues and re-entries of a single are counted together.

Rank/Single/Artist/Points

1 *You're The One That I Want* – 2694 points

2 *Xanadu* – 1817 points

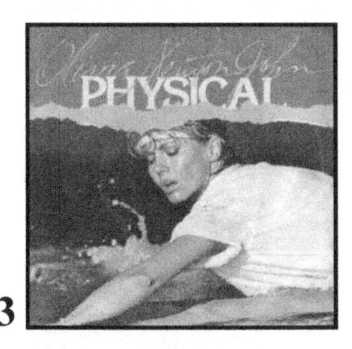

3 *Physical* – 1627 points

4 *Summer Nights* – 1560 points

Rank/Single/Artist/Points

5. *The Grease Megamix* – 1078 points

6. *A Little More Love* – 912 points
7. *Magic* – 884 points
8. *Hopelessly Devoted To You* – 800 points
8. *Heart Attack* – 800 points
10. *Twist Of Fate* – 621 points

11. *If Not For You* – 601 points
12. *I Honestly Love You* – 585 points
13. *Sam* – 536 points
14. *Banks Of The Ohio* – 531 points
14. *Make A Move On Me* – 531 points

16. *Have You Never Been Mellow* – 511 points
17. *If You Love Me (Let Me Know)* – 447 points
18. *Suddenly* – 408 points
19. *Let Me Be There* – 380 points
20. *Please Mr. Please* – 372 points

21. *Long Live Love* – 347 points
22. *Come On Over* – 298 points
23. *Soul Kiss* – 297 points
24. *Take Me Home Country Roads* – 282 points
25. *Something Better To Do* – 252 points

You're The One That I Want, predictably given its worldwide success, emerges as Olivia's most successful single, and songs from *Grease* fill three of the Top 5 places. Another collaboration from a film, *Xanadu*, takes the runner-up spot, while Olivia's highest placed solo single is *Physical*, which topped the Hot 100 in the USA for 10 weeks.

SINGLES TRIVIA

To date, Olivia has achieved 42 Top 40 singles in one or more of the countries featured in this book.

There follows a country-by-country look at Olivia's most successful hits.

Note: in the past, there was often one or more weeks over Christmas and New Year when no new chart was published in some countries. In such cases, the previous week's chart has been used to complete chart runs. Similarly, where a bi-weekly or monthly chart was in place, for chart runs these are counted as two and four weeks, respectively.

OLIVIA IN AUSTRALIA

Olivia has achieved 36 hit singles in Australia, which spent a total of 601 weeks on the chart.

No.1 Singles

1971	*Banks Of The Ohio*
1974	*I Honestly Love You*
1978	*You're The One That I Want*
1981	*Physical*
1991	*The Grease Megamix*

Most weeks at no.1

9 weeks	*You're The One That I Want*
5 weeks	*Banks Of The Ohio*
5 weeks	*Physical*
5 weeks	*The Grease Megamix*
4 weeks	*I Honestly Love You*

Singles with the most weeks

39 weeks	*Sam*
32 weeks	*You're The One That I Want*
30 weeks	*Let Me Be There*
30 weeks	*Jolene*

29 weeks   *Physical*
25 weeks   *Banks Of The Ohio*
24 weeks   *The Grease Megamix*
23 weeks   *I Honestly Love You*
22 weeks   *Long Live Love*
22 weeks   *If You Love Me (Let Me Know)*

OLIVIA IN AUSTRIA

Olivia has achieved 7 hit singles in Austria, which spent a total of 97 weeks on the chart.

No.1 Singles

1978   *Summer Nights*
1980   *Xanadu*

Most weeks at no.1

4 weeks   *Summer Nights*
4 weeks   *Xanadu*

Singles with the most weeks

40 weeks   *You're The One That I Want*
18 weeks   *Xanadu*
12 weeks   *Summer Nights*
12 weeks   *The Grease Megamix*
10 weeks   *Heart Attack*

OLIVIA IN CANADA

Olivia has achieved 32 hit singles in Canada, which have spent a total of 457 weeks on the chart.

No.1 Singles

1974   *I Honestly Love You*
1975   *Have You Never Been Mellow*
1975   *Please Mr. Please*

1978   *Hopelessly Devoted To You*
1980   *Magic*
1981   *Physical*

Most weeks at No.1

6 weeks   *Physical*
3 weeks   *Have You Never Been Mellow*
2 weeks   *Hopelessly Devoted To You*
2 weeks   *Magic*

Singles with the most weeks

29 weeks   *Physical*
23 weeks   *You're The One That I Want*
25 weeks   *I Honestly Love You*
22 weeks   *If Not For You*
22 weeks   *Magic*
21 weeks   *A Little More Love*
19 weeks   *Hopelessly Devoted To You*
19 weeks   *If You Love Me (Let Me Know)*
19 weeks   *The Best Of Me*
17 weeks   *Please Mr. Please*
17 weeks   *I Can't Help It*
17 weeks   *Heart Attack*
17 weeks   *Twist Of Fate*

Music Canada Single Certifications

2 x Platinum   *Physical* (May 1982) = 200,000
Gold   *Summer Nights* (October 1978) = 75,000
Gold   *Hopelessly Devoted To You* (October 1978) = 75,000
Gold   *A Little More Love* (May 1979) = 75,000
Gold   *Make A Move On Me* (May 1982) = 50,000
Gold   *Heart Attack* (December 1982) = 50,000
Gold   *Twist Of Fate* (January 1984) = 50,000

OLIVIA IN GERMANY

Olivia has achieved 12 hit singles in Germany, which spent a total of 163 weeks on the chart.

No.1 Singles

1978	*You're The One That I Want*
1980	*Xanadu*

Most weeks at no.1

6 weeks	*You're The One That I Want*
2 weeks	*Xanadu*

Singles with the most weeks

35 weeks	*You're The One That I Want*
29 weeks	*Xanadu*
21 weeks	*Physical*
18 weeks	*Summer Nights*
11 weeks	*Banks Of The Ohio*
10 weeks	*Magic*
10 weeks	*The Rumour*
8 weeks	*Make A Move On Me*
8 weeks	*The Grease Megamix*
6 weeks	*A Little More Love*

OLIVIA IN IRELAND

Olivia has achieved 17 hit singles in Ireland, which spent a total of 141 weeks on the chart.

No.1 Singles

1977	*Sam*
1978	*You're The One That I Want*
1978	*Summer Nights*
1978	*Hopelessly Devoted To You*
1980	*Xanadu*

Most weeks at no.1

9 weeks   *You're The One That I Want*
6 weeks   *Xanadu*
3 weeks   *Summer Nights*

Singles with the most weeks

28 weeks   *You're The One That I Want*
16 weeks   *Hopelessly Devoted To You*
15 weeks   *Summer Nights*
12 weeks   *A Little More Love*
10 weeks   *Xanadu*
 8 weeks   *Banks Of The Ohio*
 8 weeks   *Take Me Home Country Roads*
 8 weeks   *Sam*
 6 weeks   *Suddenly*
 6 weeks   *The Grease Megamix*

OLIVIA IN JAPAN

Olivia has achieved 17 hit singles in Japan, which have spent a total of 262 weeks on the chart.

Her highest charting single is *Jolene*, which achieved no.11 in 1976.

Singles with the most weeks

37 weeks   *Jolene*
33 weeks   *You're The One That I Want*
31 weeks   *Take Me Home Country Roads*
27 weeks   *Xanadu*
25 weeks   *Physical*
20 weeks   *Have You Never Been Mellow*
15 weeks   *Magic*
12 weeks   *Make A Move On Me*
11 weeks   *Compassionate Man*
11 weeks   *Twist Of Fate*

OLIVIA IN THE NETHERLANDS

Olivia has achieved 14 hit singles, which spent a total of 153 weeks on the chart, in the Netherlands.

No.1 Singles

1978	*You're The One That I Want*
1978	*Hopelessly Devoted To You*
1978	*Summer Nights*
1980	*Xanadu*

Most weeks at no.1

8 weeks	*You're The One That I Want*
5 weeks	*Xanadu*
4 weeks	*Hopelessly Devoted To You*

Singles with the most weeks

34 weeks	*You're The One That I Want*
18 weeks	*The Grease Megamix*
17 weeks	*Xanadu*
16 weeks	*Hopelessly Devoted To You*
14 weeks	*Physical*
13 weeks	*Summer Nights*
13 weeks	*A Little More Love*
9 weeks	*Grease – The Dream Mix*
6 weeks	*Magic*
6 weeks	*Soul Kiss*

OLIVIA IN NEW ZEALAND

Olivia has achieved 24 hit singles in New Zealand, which have spent 267 weeks on the chart.

No.1 Singles

1978	*You're The One That I Want*
1981	*Physical*

Most weeks at no.1

4 weeks	*You're The One That I Want*
3 weeks	*Physical*

Singles with the most weeks

27 weeks	*You're The One That I Want*
22 weeks	*Come On Over*
18 weeks	*Physical*
16 weeks	*Magic*
16 weeks	*Heart Attack*
14 weeks	*Have You Never Been Mellow*
14 weeks	*Please Mr. Please*
14 weeks	*The Grease Megamix*
13 weeks	*Let Me Be There*
13 weeks	*Hopelessly Devoted To You*
13 weeks	*A Little More Love*

OLIVIA IN NORWAY

Olivia has achieved 8 hit singles in Norway, which have spent 99 weeks on the chart.

No.1 Singles

1978	*You're The One That I Want*
1980	*Xanadu*

Most weeks at no.1

18 weeks	*You're The One That I Want*
6 weeks	*Xanadu*

Singles with the most weeks

30 weeks	*You're The One That I Want*
14 weeks	*Summer Nights*
14 weeks	*Xanadu*
12 weeks	*If Not For You*
12 weeks	*Long Live Love*

OLIVIA IN SOUTH AFRICA

Olivia has achieved 8 hit singles in South Africa, which spent a total of 72 weeks on the chart.

Olivia's most successful single is *You're The One That I Want*, which peaked at no.2.

Singles with the most weeks

18 weeks	*You're The One That I Want*
12 weeks	*Heart Attack*
10 weeks	*Twist Of Fate*
9 weeks	*Every Face Tells A Story*
9 weeks	*Magic*

OLIVIA IN SPAIN

Olivia has achieved six singles in Spain, which have spent 94 weeks on the chart.

No.1 Singles

1978	*You're The One That I Want*
1980	*Xanadu*
1991	*The Grease Megamix*

Most weeks at No.1

12 weeks	*The Grease Megamix*
8 weeks	*You're The One That I Want*
6 weeks	*Xanadu*

Singles with the most weeks

25 weeks	*You're The One That I Want*
25 weeks	*The Grease Megamix*
24 weeks	*Xanadu*
10 weeks	*Physical*
7 weeks	*I Can't Help It*

OLIVIA IN SWEDEN

Olivia has achieved 6 hit singles in Sweden, which have spent 102 weeks on the chart.

No.1 Singles

1978   *You're The One That I Want*

You're The One That I Want topped the chart for 12 weeks.

Singles with the most weeks

34 weeks	*You're The One That I Want*
24 weeks	*Xanadu*
20 weeks	*Summer Nights*
12 weeks	*A Little More Love*
8 weeks	*Physical*

OLIVIA IN SWITZERLAND

Olivia has achieved 5 hit singles in Switzerland, which have spent 66 weeks on the chart.

No.1 Singles

1978	*You're The One That I Want*
1981	*Physical*

Most weeks at no.1

7 weeks	*You're The One That I Want*
4 weeks	*Physical*

Singles with the most weeks

24 weeks	*You're The One That I Want*
14 weeks	*Xanadu*
12 weeks	*Physical*
10 weeks	*Summer Nights*
6 weeks	*Twist Of Fate*

OLIVIA IN THE UK

Olivia has achieved 27 Top 100 singles, which have spent a total of 246 weeks on the chart in the UK.

No.1 Singles

1978	*You're The One That I Want*
1978	*Summer Nights*
1980	*Xanadu*

Olivia's most successful solo single is *Hopelessly Devoted To You*, which peaked at no.2.

Most weeks at no.1

9 weeks	*You're The One That I Want*
7 weeks	*Summer Nights*
2 weeks	*Xanadu*

Singles with the most weeks

37 weeks	*You're The One That I Want*
19 weeks	*Summer Nights*
17 weeks	*Banks Of The Ohio*
17 weeks	*Physical*
13 weeks	*Take Me Home Country Roads*
12 weeks	*A Little More Love*
12 weeks	*The Grease Megamix*
11 weeks	*If Not For You*
11 weeks	*I Honestly Love You*
11 weeks	*Sam*
11 weeks	*Hopelessly Devoted To You*
11 weeks	*Xanadu*

BPI (British Phonographic Industry) Awards

The BPI began certifying Silver, Gold & Platinum singles in 1973. From 1973 to 1988: Silver = 250,000, Gold = 500,000 & Platinum = 1 million. From 1989 onwards: Silver = 200,000, Gold = 400,000 & Platinum = 600,000. Awards are based on shipments, not sales; however, in July 2013 the BPI automated awards, based on actual sales since February 1994.

Platinum   *You're The One That I Want* (July 1978) = 1 million
Gold   *Summer Nights* (October 1978) = 500,000
Gold   *Hopelessly Devoted To You* (November 1978) = 500,000
Silver   *A Little More Love* (November 1978) = 250,000
Silver   *Xanadu* (July 1980) = 250,000
Silver   *Physical* (December 1981) = 250,000

You're The One That I Want has sold over 2 million copies in the UK, while *Summer Nights* has sold around 1.6 million copies.

OLIVIA IN THE USA

Olivia has achieved 38 hit singles in the USA, which have spent a total of 526 weeks on the Hot 100.

No.1 Singles

1974	*I Honestly Love You*
1975	*Have You Never Been Mellow*
1978	*You're The One That I Want*
1980	*Magic*
1981	*Physical*

Most weeks at no.1

10 weeks	*Physical*
4 weeks	*Magic*
2 weeks	*I Honestly Love You*

Singles with the most Hot 100 weeks

36 weeks	*I Honestly Love You*
27 weeks	*Physical*
24 weeks	*You're The One That I Want*
23 weeks	*Magic*
21 weeks	*Heart Attack*
20 weeks	*If You Love Me (Let Me Know)*
20 weeks	*A Little More Love*
20 weeks	*One Heart At A Time*
19 weeks	*Let Me Be There*

19 weeks   *Hopelessly Devoted To You*
19 weeks   *Suddenly*

One Heart At A Time, which peaked at no.56, was credited to Olivia Newton-John, Faith Hill, Garth Brooks, Bryan White & Michael McDonald.

RIAA (Recording Industry Association of America) Awards

The RIAA began certifying Gold singles in 1958 and Platinum singles in 1976. From 1958 to 1988: Gold = 1 million, Platinum = 2 million. From 1988 onwards: Gold = 500,000, Platinum = 1 million. Awards are based on shipments, not sales (unless the award is for digital sales, which none of Olivia's awards are).

Platinum	*You're The One That I Want* (July 1978)	= 2 million
Platinum	*Physical* (January 1982)	= 2 million
Gold	*Let Me Be There* (February 1974)	= 1 million
Gold	*If You Love Me (Let Me Know)* (June 1974)	= 1 million
Gold	*I Honestly Love You* (October 1974)	= 1 million
Gold	*Have You Never Been Mellow* (March 1975)	= 1 million
Gold	*Please Mr. Please* (September 1975)	= 1 million
Gold	*Hopelessly Devoted To You* (August 1978)	= 1 million
Gold	*Summer Nights* (August 1978)	= 1 million
Gold	*A Little More Love* (February 1979)	= 1 million
Gold	*Magic* (July 1980)	= 1 million

All The Top 40 Albums

1 ~ IF NOT FOR YOU / OLIVIA NEWTON-JOHN

Me And Bobby McGee/If/Banks Of The Ohio/In A Station/Love Song/Help Me Make It Through The Night/If Not For You/Where Are You Going To My Love?/Lullaby/If I Could Read Your Mind/If I Gotta Leave/No Regrets

Produced by Bruce Welch & John Farrar.

Australia: Interfusion SITFL-934320 (as *IF NOT FOR YOU*, 1971).

13.12.71: peaked at no.**14**, charted for 12 weeks

UK: Pye International NSPL 28155 (as *OLIVIA NEWTON-JOHN*, 1971).

OLIVIA NEWTON-JOHN wasn't a hit in the UK.

Born in England, raised in Australia, Olivia returned to England, to try find success in the music business. Her debut album, recorded at London's Abbey Road Studios during 1971, was produced by John Farrar, who went on to work with Olivia for the next decade and a half, and her boyfriend at the time, Bruce Welch. Farrar and Welch, along with Hank Marvin, formed the trio Marvin, Welch and Farrar, although Marvin and Welch are far better known as member of The Shadows, who enjoyed success as Cliff Richard's backing band and in their own right.

The album was titled *IF NOT FOR YOU* in most countries, but simply *OLIVIA NEWTON-JOHN* in the UK. As well as a version of the 'murder ballad' *Banks Of The Ohio*, the album comprised covers of contemporary 1960s and early 1970s songs, including Bob Dylan's *If Not For You*, Roger Miller's *Me And Bobby McGee*, David Gates's *If*, Gordon Lightfoot's *If You Could Read My Mind* and Kris Kristofferson's *Help Me Make It Through The Night*.

Olivia promoted the album by making guest appearances on numerous TV shows across Europe and Australia, and she appeared on *The Dean Martin Show* in the USA. In 1972, she toured with Cliff Richard, on The Cliff Richard / If Not For You Tour. Despite this, the only country where the album was a hit was Australia, where it achieved no.14. The album did yield two hit singles, *If Not For You* and *Banks Of The Ohio*.

Olivia recorded three songs for the album that failed to make the final cut. The first, *The Biggest Clown*, was released as the B-side of her *If Not For You* single. *Would You Follow Me* was released as the B-side of *Banks Of The Ohio* single in some countries, including the UK. The third, *It's Hard To Say Goodbye*, was released as the B-side of *Love Songs*, which was only issued as a single in Germany and the UK, and wasn't a hit.

It's Hard To Say Goodbye and *Would You Follow Me* both featured on Olivia's 1994 2CD compilation, *48 ORIGINAL TRACKS*.

2 ~ LET ME BE THERE

Let Me Be There/Me And Bobby McGee/Banks Of The Ohio/Love Song/If Not For You/ Take Me Home Country Roads/Angel Of The Morning/If You Could Read My Mind/Help Me Make It Through The Night/Just A Little Too Much

Australia & UK: Not Released.

USA: MCA MCA-389 (1973).

26.01.74: 99-76-72-68-58-55-**54**-56-66-93

Canada
16.02.74: 86-71-50-**39**-51-70-74-78-78
10.05.75: 97-95-90-82-91

Japan
20.12.74: peaked at no.**25**, charted for 44 weeks

Olivia's second album, titled simply *OLIVIA*, wasn't a hit, but this North American compilation that followed in late 1973 was.
    The title track apart, which gave Olivia her first Top 10 single in the USA, all the tracks on the album had featured on Olivia's first two albums. The album sleeve featured the same photograph of Olivia, taken during one of her concerts in Japan, as her *OLIVIA* album.

The album achieved Top 40 status in Canada and Japan, where it rose to no.39 and no.25, respectively, but fell short in the USA, where it peaked at no.54.

3 ~ LET ME BE THERE / MUSIC MAKES MY DAY

Take Me Home Country Road/Amoureuse/Brotherly Love/Heartbreaker/Rosewater/You Ain't Got The Right/Feeling Best/Being On The Losing End/Let Me Be There/Music Makes My Day/Leaving/If We Try

Produced by John Farrar; except *Brotherly Love*, produced by Bruce Welch & *Music Makes My Day*, produced by John Farrar, Bruce Welch & Alan Hawkshaw.

Australia: Interfusion L35026 (1974).

LET ME BE THERE wasn't a hit in Australia.

UK: Pye International NSPL 28185 (1973).

2.03.74: 38-48
20.04.74: **37**

As with her debut, Olivia released this album with two different titles: *LET ME BE THERE* in Australia and *MUSIC MAKES MY DAY* in the UK. All the songs on the album – some previously released – were cover versions, apart from the title track.

    LET ME BE THERE wasn't a hit in Australia, but *MUSIC MAKES MY DAY* gave Olivia her first hit album in the UK, where it achieved no.37.

The new album from
Olivia
Newton-John
'Music
Makes
My Day'
NSPL 28185
PYE
Also available on Precision Tapes Cassettes & Cartridges

4 ~ IF YOU LOVE ME LET ME KNOW

If You Love Me (Let Me Know)/Mary Skeffington/Country Girl/I Honestly Love You/Free The People/The River's Too Wide/Home Ain't Home Anymore/God Only Knows/Changes/ You Ain't Got The Right

Produced by John Farrar, except *Mary Skeffington & Changes*, produced by Bruce Welch.

Australia & UK: Not Released.

USA: MCA MCA-411 (1974).

15.06.74: 99-55-32-29-23-20-17-14-11-26-29-24-21-6-5-4-2-**1**-4-20-23-45-65-69-83-88

Canada
22.06.74: 97-64-39-32-24-18-15-13-12-19-24-22-21-9-7-3-**1**-2-4-14-23-18-26-34-54-66
10.05.75: 94-75-72-60-63-77-79-71-70-65-60-59-63-70-84

This album, released exclusively in North America, was once again effectively a compilation, with only the title track being new: six tracks were cherry-picked from Olivia's *LONG LIVE LOVE* album, which was released at around the same time, with two tracks from *OLIVIA* and one from *MUSIC MAKES MY DAY* completing the track listing.

Boosted by the success of *I Honestly Love You*, a no.1 in Canada and the USA, *IF YOU LOVE ME LET ME KNOW* followed suit, and topped the album chart in both countries.

5 ~ LONG LIVE LOVE

Free The People/Angel Eyes/Country Girl/Someday/God Only Knows/Loving You Ain't Easy/Home Ain't Home Anymore/Have Love Will Travel/I Honestly Love You/Hands Across The Sea/The River's Too Wide/Long Live Love

Produced by John Farrar.

Australia: Interfusion L35230 (1974).

30.09.74: peaked at no.**19**, charted for 24 weeks

UK: EMI EMC 3028 (1974).

29.06.74: **40-x-44**

The 1974 Eurovision Song Contest was staged at The Dome in Brighton, England, on 6th April 1974. The BBC had agreed to take on the contest after – following victories in 1972 and 1973 – Luxembourg declined, due to the cost of staging the event.

Olivia was chosen as the UK's representative, and followed her good friend Cliff Richard, who had come third in the 1973 contest with *Power To All Our Friends*. Olivia presented six songs on Jimmy Saville's *Clunk Click* TV show, and on 23rd February 1974 it was revealed on *A Song For Europe 1974* the public had voted *Long Live Love* as the song that would represent the UK – not a view Olivia shared, as her personal favourite was

Angel Eyes. Long Live Love came joint fourth at the Eurovision Song Contest, with the then virtually unknown ABBA taking the top prize with *Waterloo*.

Olivia recorded all six songs that were nominated for the Eurovision Song Contest, and they all featured on an album titled after the UK's winning song, *Long Live Love*. The albums highlight, however, was *I Honestly Love You*, which gave Olivia her first chart topping single in North America.

In Japan, *LONG LIVE LOVE* featured two bonus tracks, *Mon Amour, Mon Impossible Amour* and a German language recording of *Long Live Love*.

6 ~ FIRST IMPRESSIONS

Australia: *If Not For You/Banks Of The Ohio/Winterwood/Take Me Home Country Roads/Amoureuse/Let Me Be There/I Love You, I Honestly Love You/Long Live Love/If You Love Me (Let Me Know)/What Is Life/If We Try/Music Makes My Day*

UK: *If Not For You/Banks Of The Ohio/Love Song/Winterwood/Everything I Own/What Is Life/Take Me Home Country Roads/Amoureuse/Let Me Be There/Changes/Music Makes My Day/If You Love Me (Let Me Know)*

Australia: Interfusion L35375 (1974).

10.02.75: peaked at no.**3**, charted for 46 weeks

UK: EMI EMC 3055 (1974).

FIRST IMPRESSIONS wasn't a hit in the UK.

New Zealand
2.05.75: 8-9-7-12-10-13-18-18-22-16-18-18-4-3-3-4-4-3-5-5-5-7-3-3-**2**-5-5-9-10-8-8-12-13-10-10-10-10-10-10-14-13-14-21-25-29-38-37-x-38-31-x-x-9-14-17-21-27-35-24-25-22-28-40-30-34-37-26-36-30-34-23-23-32-x-27-x-x-24-34-35-17-x-38-32-33-18
20.02.77: 31-35

Less than four years after she released her debut album, Olivia had accumulated enough hits and popular tracks to justify her first greatest hits compilation, *FIRST IMPRESSIONS*.

In Australia and New Zealand, the album was sub-titled 'great hits!', and was a major success, rising to no.3 and no.2, respectively, and charting for the best part of a year in Australia and well over a year in New Zealand.

The album was less well received in other countries, including the UK, where the compilation was released with a slightly different track listing.

7 ~ HAVE YOU NEVER BEEN MELLOW

Have You Never Been Mellow/Loving Arms/Lifestream/Goodbye Again/Water Under The Bridge/I Never Did Sing You A Love Song/It's So Easy/The Air That I Breathe/Follow Me/And In The Morning/Please Mr. Please/If You Love Me (Let Me Know)

Produced by John Farrar.

Australia: Interfusion L35465 (1975).

26.05.75: peaked at no.**13**, charted for 22 weeks

UK: EMI EMC 3069 (1975).

26.04.75: **37**-x-47

Canada
8.03.75: 97-21-6-**3**-**3**-5-6-4-5-8-7-10-19-30-30-35-38-64-63-75-65-49-44-42-38-37-33-38-51-90-82-78
13.12.75: 95-79-76-67-70-x-x-x-98

Japan
20.04.75: peaked at no.**4**, charted for 48 weeks

New Zealand
27.06.75: 39-29-34-37-30-**20**-34-33-33-32-37-33-x-36

USA
22.02.75: 43-10-3-**1**-2-2-2-3-4-3-4-4-6-11-15-28-41-60-67-72-88-77-66-55-43-38-38-42

Recorded in 1974, and released in early 1975, *HAVE YOU NEVER BEEN MELLOW* continued Olivia's run of success in Australasia and North America, as well as giving Olivia a major hit in Japan.

In North America, where it had already been released on the similarly titled album, *If You Love Me (Let Me Know)* was omitted from the track listing. This didn't stop the album from going all the way to no.1 in the USA, and to no.3 in Canada. The album peaked at no.4 in Japan where, when the album was reissued on CD in 1998, *I Honestly Love You* featured as the album's twelfth and last track, rather than *If You Love Me (Let Me Know)*.

The album was less successful in Australia and New Zealand, but achieved no.13 and no.20, respectively, and charted for five months in Australia.

Two singles – the title track and *Please Mr. Please* – were released from the album, and were both big hits in North America, where *Have You Never Been Mellow* gave Olivia another chart topping single in the USA. In the UK, however, neither single charted, and as a consequence the album struggled, making its chart debut at no.37 but rising no higher.

8 ~ CLEARLY LOVE

Something Better To Do/Lovers/Slow Down Jackson/He's My Rock/Sail Into Tomorrow/ Crying, Laughing, Loving, Lying/Clearly Love/Let It Shine/Summertime Blues/Just A Lot Of Folk (The Marshmellow Song)/He Ain't Heavy ... He's My Brother

Produced by John Farrar.

Australia: Interfusion L35704 (1975).

24.11.75: peaked at no.**50**, charted for 16 weeks

UK: EMI EMA 774 (1975).

CLEARLY LOVE wasn't a hit in the UK.

Canada
18.10.75: 88-70
13.12.75: 80-70-41-**39**-51-x-x-x-80
17.07.76: 87-82-90-83-79-71-66-64-60-56-89

Japan
20.11.75: peaked at no.**3**, charted for 30 weeks

New Zealand
27.02.76: 37-**34**-37

USA
11.10.75: 49-29-19-16-**12-12**-13-41-61

Recorded at EMI Studios in London, England, *CLEARLY LOVE* featured both new songs and cover versions, the latter including Eddie Cochran's *Summertime Blues* and the Hollies hit, *He Ain't Heavy ... He's My Brother*.

   The album charted highest in Japan, where it peaked at no.3, but it failed to make the Top 10 in most other countries. In the USA, where Olivia's two previous studio albums both went to no.1, *CLEARLY LOVE* could only manage no.12, and elsewhere the album charted at no.34 in New Zealand, no.39 in Canada and no.50 in Australia. The album failed to chart in the UK.

Two singles were lifted from the album, *Something Better To Do* and *He Ain't Heavy ... He's My Brother* b/w *Let It Shine*. Although neither was a huge hit, both did achieve Top 40 status, with *Let It Shine* being preferred to Olivia's cover of *He Ain't Heavy ... He's My Brother* where the single charted; both songs were listed on the Hot 100 in the USA.

9 ~ COME ON OVER

Jolene/Pony Ride/Come On Over/It'll Be Me/Greensleeves/Blue Eyes Crying In The Rain/Don't Throw It All Away/Who Are You Now?/Smile For Me/Small Talk And Pride/Wrap Me In Your Arms/The Long And Winding Road

Produced by John Farrar.

Australia: Interfusion L35847 (1976).

3.05.76: peaked at no.**29**, charted for 17 weeks

UK: EMI EMC 3124 (1976).

29.05.76: 50-53-**49**-60

Canada
24.04.76: 99-56-35-**30**-41-41-48-92-70-70

Japan
20.04.76: peaked at no.**2**, charted for 72 weeks

New Zealand
9.07.76: **12**-12-14-16-15-17-13-15-18-16-22-14-18-23-40-30-35-x-33

OLIVIA NEWTON-JOHN
Her newest album
Produced by John Farrar
COME ON OVER
includes
Don't Throw It All Away
COME ON OVER
MCA RECORDS

USA
20.03.76: 97-39-27-20-18-16-14-14-**13**-19-27-44-76-76-93

Like *CLEARLY LOVE, COME ON OVER* featured a mix of new songs and cover versions. The title track was a Bee Gees song, and the album also included covers of Dolly Parton's *Jolene* and Lennon & McCartney's *The Long And Winding Road*, plus the traditional song, *Greensleeves*, which Olivia adapted and arranged herself.

In Japan, where *Jolene* gave Olivia her biggest hit single, *COME ON OVER* was a major success, and peaked at no.2. The album couldn't repeat this success elsewhere, but it did chart higher than *CLEARLY LOVE* in most countries, and achieved no.12 in New Zealand, no.13 in the USA, no.29 in Australia and no.30 in Canada. The album also broke Olivia's run of misses in the UK, where it spent a month on the chart and rose to no.49.

Come On Over
一人ぽっちの囁き

In most countries, excluding Japan, the only single released from *COME ON OVER* was the title track, which enjoyed moderate success.

10 ~ CRYSTAL LADY

LP1: *If Not For You/It's So Hard To Say Goodbye/Would You Follow Me/I'm A Small And Lonely Light/Banks Of The Ohio/Where Are You Going To My Love/Just A Little Too Much/Maybe Then I'll Think Of You/Me And Bobby McGee/If/In A Station/Help Me Make It Through The Night/Lullaby/If You Could Read My Mind/If I Gotta Leave/Take Me Home Country Roads*

LP2: *If We Only Have Love/My Old Man's Got A Gun/Mary Skeffington/Angel Of The Morning/Why Don't You Write Me/Behind That Locked Door/Living In Harmony/I Will Touch You/Heartbreaker/Rosewater/Feeling Best/Being On The Losing End/You Ain't Got The Right/Leaving/Let Me Be There/If We Try*

Australia & UK: Not Released.

Japan: EMI EMS 65001-2 (1976).

5.10.76: peaked at no.**16**, charted for 26 weeks

This compilation, a double album, was released exclusively in Japan, where it rose to no.16 and spent six months on the chart.

11 ~ DON'T STOP BELIEVIN'

Don't Stop Believin'/A Thousand Conversations/Compassionate Man/New-Born Babe/ Hey Mr. Dreammaker/Every Face Tells A Story/Sam/Love You Hold The Key/I'll Bet You A Kangaroo/The Last Time You Loved

Produced by John Farrar.

Australia: Interfusion L39023 (1976).

6.12.76: peaked at no.**88**, charted for 6 weeks

UK: EMI EMC 3162 (1976).

DON'T STOP BELIEVIN' wasn't a hit in the UK.

Canada
13.11.76: ?-79-72-60-58-**56**-57-57-69-73-77-86-92

Japan
25.11.76: peaked at no.**3**, charted for 26 weeks

USA
6.11.76: 69-51-41-37-34-**30-30**-64-64-62-62-62-56-50-61-66-71-88-98-89-86-94-94

DON'T STOP BELIEVIN' was the first album Olivia recorded in the home of country music, Nashville, Tennessee.

Once again, the album was a major hit in Japan, where it achieved no.3, but sales were generally disappointing in other countries. The album charted at no.30 in the USA, no.56 in Canada and a lowly no.88 in Australia, and like most of Olivia's recent albums it failed to chart in the UK.

The title track was one of four singles released from the album, although *Compassionate Man* was only issued in Japan, where it was chosen ahead of Olivia's cover of the Cliff Richard hit, *Every Face Tells A Story*. Unusually, the last single lifted from the album – *Sam* – proved to be the most successful, especially in the UK where it returned Olivia to the Top 10.

12 ~ MAKING A GOOD THING BETTER

Making A Good Thing Better/Slow Dancing/Ring Of Fire/Coolin' Down/Don't Cry For Me Argentina/Sad Songs/You Won't See Me Cry/So Easy To Begin/I Think I'll Say Goodbye/Don't Ask A Friend/If Love Is Real

Produced by John Farrar.

Australia: Interfusion L36277 (1977).

22.08.77: peaked at no.**71**, charted for 14 weeks

UK: EMI EMC 3192 (1977).

27.08.77: **60**

Canada
30.07.77: 100-93-81-60-37-**33**-41-63-71-85

Japan
20.07.77: peaked at no.**3**, charted for 17 weeks

USA
16.07.77: 88-75-49-49-46-41-37-36-36-**34**-45-75

OLIVIA NEWTON-JOHN
Making a good thing better

Generally considered to be Olivia's 10th studio album, *MAKING A GOOD THING BETTER* was also her penultimate solo album of the 1970s. More significantly, it was also the last album she released, before she signed on to make a film co-starring John Travolta: *Grease*.

At the time of the album's release, Olivia was in dispute with her record company, MCA Records, claiming they weren't promoting her music, which had resulted in declining sales. Consequently, MCA didn't promote *MAKING A GOOD THING BETTER*, and although Olivia performed the title track on NBC's *Midnight Special* and appeared on the cover of *US Weekly* magazine, the album didn't sell well.

The album did achieve Top 40 status in Canada and the USA, where it peaked at no.33 and no.34, respectively, but it was only a minor hit in Australia and the UK.

The album's title track and Olivia's cover of *Don't Cry For Me Argentina*, from the Tim Rice & Andrew Lloyd Webber musical opera *Evita*, were released as singles in select countries. *Don't Cry For Me Argentina* was a Top 40 hit in Australia, but *Making A Good Thing Better* wasn't a hit anywhere.

13 ~ GREATEST HITS VOLUME 2 / GREATEST HITS

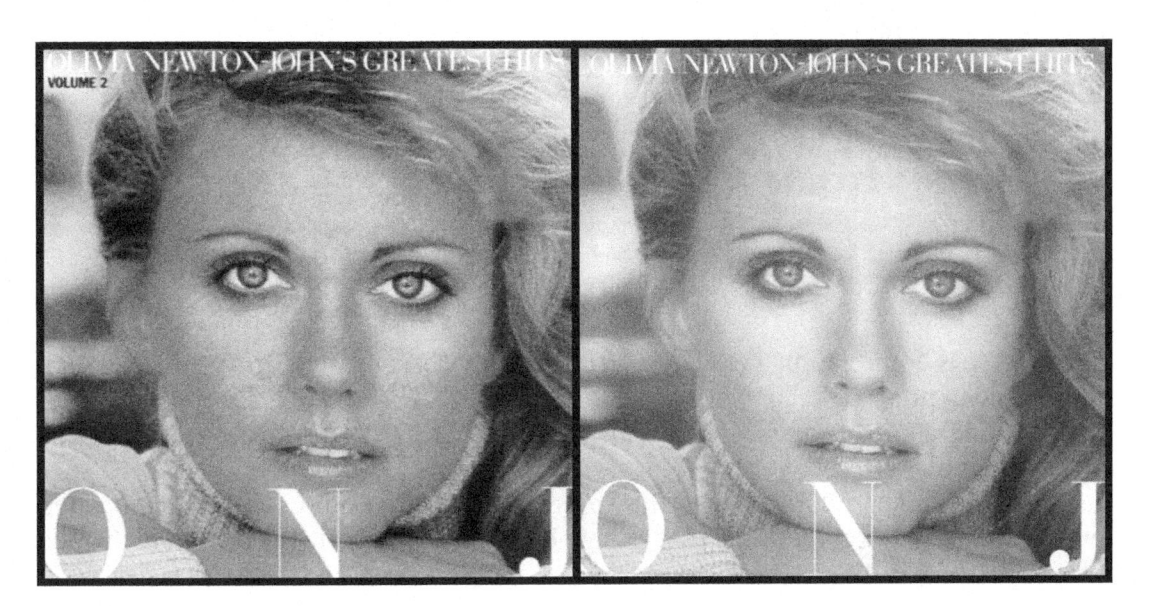

Australia: *Changes/Every Face Tells A Story/Let It Shine/Come On Over/Love Song/Have You Never Been Mellow/Don't Cry For Me Argentina/Please Mr. Please/Something Better To Do/ Jolene/The Air That I Breathe/Don't Stop Believin'/Making A Good Thing Better/Sam*

UK: *Changes/If Not For You/Let Me Be There/If You Love Me (Let Me Know)/I Honestly Love You/Have You Never Been Mellow/Please Mr. Please/Take Me Home Country Roads/Let It Shine/Banks Of The Ohio/Don't Stop Believin'/Sam*

Australia: Interfusion L36449 (1977).

12.12.77: peaked at no.**18**, charted for 75 weeks

UK: EMI EMA 785 (1977).

21.01.78: 24-24-20-23-**19**-31-48-x-53-x-x-x-43

Canada
26.11.77: 84-78-45-24-12-12-12-12-**11-11-11**-21-36-48-56-78-94-97-98

Japan
5.01.77: peaked at no.**5**, charted for 29 weeks

145

Netherlands
4.11.78: 36-**24**-25-38-46-34-41
19.03.94: 81-48-31-29-33-33-37-40-46-64-72

New Zealand
26.02.78: 37
9.07.78: 23-12-11-12-16-13-26-26-24-34-23-x-37-x-38-37-x-43-**10**-19-25-26-37-39

USA
12.11.77: 38-34-27-25-19-17-16-16-14-**13-13**-18-34-54-93

In Australia, Olivia's compilation *FIRST IMPRESSIONS* was sub-titled 'great hits!', which led to this greatest hits package being titled *GREATEST HITS VOLUME 2*. In other countries, including North America where *FIRST IMPRESSIONS* wasn't released, the album was titled simply *GREATEST HITS*.

The track listing in Australia and the UK varied slightly, but both compilations opened with *Changes*, the only track included that hadn't been issued as a single. *Changes*, which Olivia composed herself, originally featured on her *IF YOU LOVE ME LET ME KNOW* album.

In Australia, although it rose no higher than no.18, *GREATEST HITS VOLUME 2* spent an impressive 75 weeks on the charts. The album achieved no.5 in Japan, no.10 in New Zealand, no.11 in Canada, no.13 in the USA, no.19 in the UK and no.24 in the Netherlands.

14 ~ GREASE

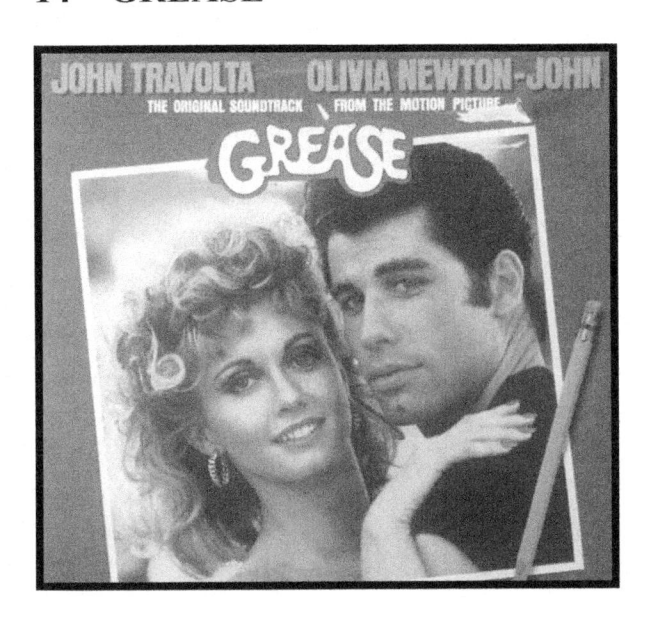

LP1: *Grease* ~ Frankie Valli
Summer Nights ~ John Travolta & Olivia Newton-John
Hopelessly Devoted To You ~ Olivia Newton-John
You're The One That I Want ~ John Travolta & Olivia Newton-John
Sandy ~ John Travolta
Beauty School Drop-Out ~ Frankie Avalon
Look At Me, I'm Sandra Dee ~ Stockard Channing
Greased Lightnin' ~ John Travolta
It's Raining On Prom Night ~ Cindy Bullens
Alone At The Drive-In Movie (Instrumental)
Blue Moon ~ Sha-Na-Na

LP2: *Rock N' Roll Is Here To Stay* ~ Sha-Na-Na
Those Magic Changes ~ Sha-Na-Na
Hound Dog ~ Sha-Na-Na
Born To Hand-Jive ~ Sha-Na-Na
Tears On My Pillow ~ Sha-Na-Na
Mooning ~ Louis St. Louis & Cindy Bullens
Freddy, My Love ~ Cindy Bullens
Rock N' Roll Party Queen ~ Louis St. Louis
There Are Worse Things I Could Do ~ Stockard Channing
Look At Me, I'm Sandra Dee (Reprise) ~ Olivia Newton-John
We Go Together ~ John Travolta & Olivia Newton-John

Love Is A Many Splendored Thing (Instrumental)
Grease (Reprise) ~ Frankie Valli

Produced by Louis St. Louis, John Farrar, Barry Gibb, Albhy Galuten & Karl Richardson.

Australia: RSO 2658 125 (1978).

5.06.78: peaked at no.**1** (11 weeks), charted for 101 weeks

UK: RSO RSD 2001 (1978).

8.07.78: 36-21-13-9-10-8-5-6-3-4-5-5-3-**1-1-1-1-1-1-1-1-1-1-1-1-1**-2-4-7-6-8-13-16-15-23-28-38-42-39-54-44-63-46-67-61-56-64

Austria
15.08.78: 5-4-5-**1-1**-3-5-9-23 (monthly)
26.07.98: 11-15-11-10-11-11-19-18-17-29-20-21-36-35-39-35

Canada
3.06.78: 89-32-20-14-10-9-9-9-9-4-**1-1-1-1-1-1-1**-2-4-3-5-6-6-6-8-8-18-20-25-40-48-48-48-48-49-53-55-56-78-87-96-98

Germany
1.08.78: 28-11-8-6-6-4-3-2-2-**1-1-1-1-1**-2-2-2-1-2-**1-1-1-1-1**-3-4-5-11-18-27-26-31-40-40-42

Japan
21.07.78: peaked at no.**1** (3 weeks), charted for 30 weeks

Netherlands
24.06.78: 19-15-13-8-5-4-4-4-3-2-2-**1-1-1-1-1-1-1-1-1-1-1-1**-2-2-2-2-2-6-2-4-10-8-16-27-22-38-40-44-48-49-45
9.03.91: 16-**8**-**1-1**-2-3-4-4-3-2-2-2-3-4-12-18-23-30-50-61-86-98-99
8.11.97: 52-57-73-73-80-94
7.02.98: 88-85-86-95
20.06.98: 75-58-27-25-21-24-18-16-19-30-34-39-48-49-24-26-80-95-95-x-x-x-72-50-60-72-82
21.08.99: 88-72-69-77-88
30.03.02: 90-92-90-80-74

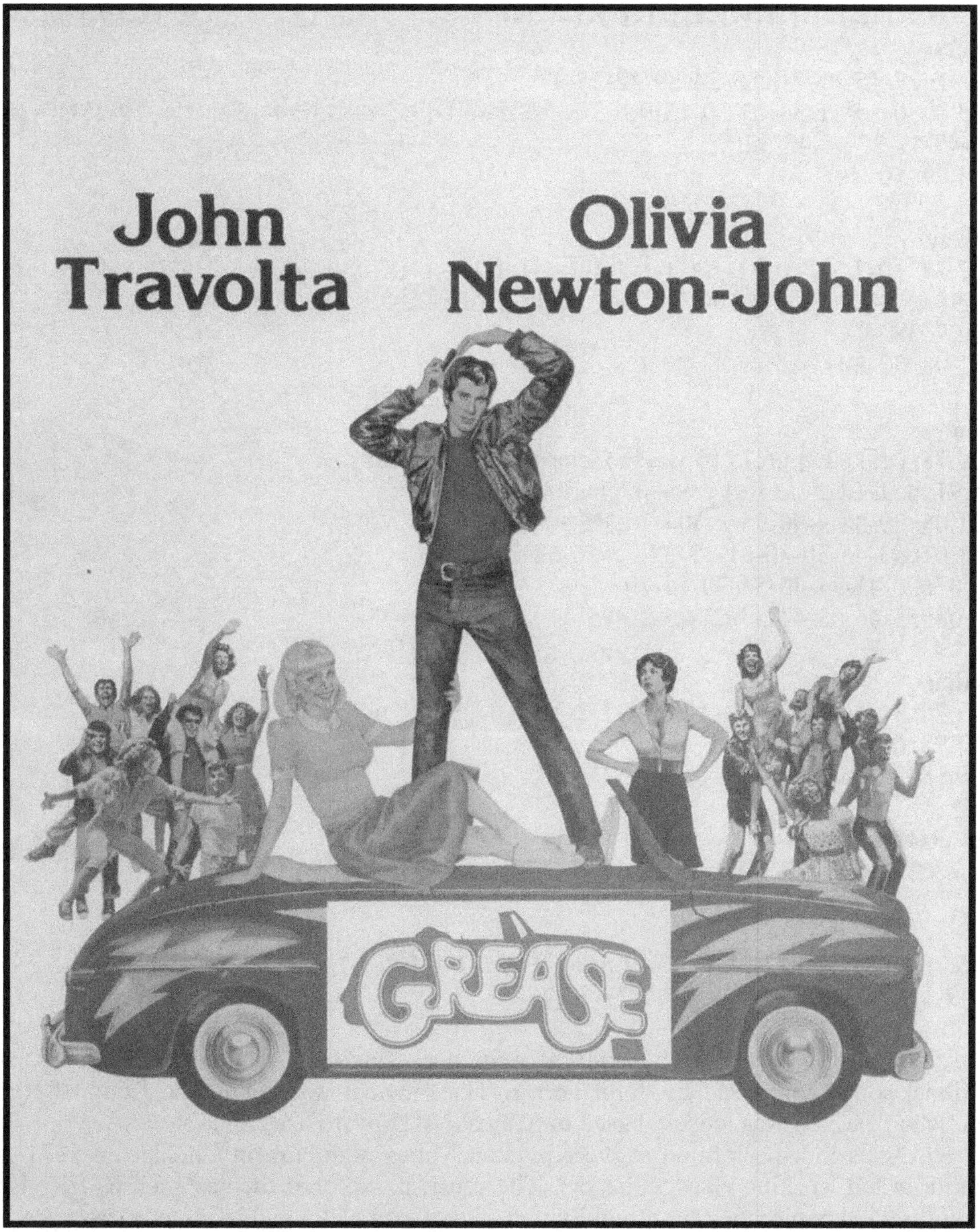
John
Travolta
Olivia
Newton-John
GREASE

New Zealand
6.08.78: 3-**1-1-1**-2-**1-1-1-1-1-1-1-1-1-1-1-1-1**-2-3-3-3-3-3-6-12-10-22-11-14-15-17-20-22-32-33
7.07.91: 27-15-11-7-11-9-24-29-42-35-47
7.06.98: 30-25-41-34-13-20-15-9-6-3-3-5-8-8-4-4-11-5-4-4-5-24-13-30-16-19-25-20-25-32-45-47-27-46-42-32
28.03.99: 50

Norway
29.07.78: 10-7-3-3-3-2-**1-1-1-1-1-1-1-1-1-1-1-1-1-1**-2-2-2-2-2-3-3-3-3-4-7
6.06.98: 27-4-2-**1-1**-2-6-10-13-13-12-11-15-16-25-22-29-30
5.06.99: 38
15.11.08: 32-27

Spain
25.09.78: peaked at no.1 (15 weeks), charted for 31 weeks
6.05.91: peaked at no.1 (4 weeks), charted for 36 weeks
16.01.05: 29-38-x-90-95-x-90
14.01.07: 53-46-50-30-31-33-32-42-56-68-73-57-73
9.09.07: 90-41-34-40-54-70-74-79
3.02.08: 53-46-63-44-59-62-75-99-95

Sweden
28.07.78: 30-10-8-3-**1-1-1-1-1-1-1-1**-2-2-5-10-15-23-30-32 (bi-weekly)
17.07.98: 60-57-x-x-42
24.09.98: 27-26-31-43-43-x-58

Switzerland
1.08.78: 10-15-6-5-3-**1-1-1-1-1-1-1**-7-9-17 (bi-weekly)

USA
20.05.78: 53-39-33-27-21-17-14-9-8-2-**1-1-1-1-1-1-1**-4-**1-1**-2-**1-1-1**-2-3-5-5-5-6-6-5-5-5-10-9-11-15-24-30-41-41-55-60-73-73-72-92-96

Grease started life as a raunchy musical written by Jim Jacobs and Warren Casey, with additional songs composed by John Farrar. The musical was set in the fictional Rydell High School, which was loosely based on Chicago's Howard Taft School.

Grease was first performed at the Kingston Mines nightclub in Chicago in 1971, and focused on ten working class teenagers. The musical explored themes such as friendship, love and sexual exploration, and highlighted social issues like gang violence, peer pressure and teenage pregnancy. The musical opened on Broadway in 1972, and at London's West

End the following year, but later performances were significantly toned down, compared with the original version.

The film rights to *Grease* were purchased by Allan Carr. John Travolta, an up-and-coming actor who was in the middle of shooting *Saturday Night Fever*, was cast in the lead male role, but Carr was struggling to find his lead female. Several actresses auditioned for the part, but only three of them were seriously considered. One, Marie Osmond, was a singer but she had little acting experience. The other two, Cheryl Ladd and Deborah Raffin, were actresses who weren't really known for their singing.

Carr was still looking for his leading lady when he was invited to a dinner party hosted by singer Helen Reddy and her husband, Jeff Wald. Olivia, a good friend of Helen Rdeey's, was invited to the same dinner party, and Carr was immediately struck by her natural beauty, but he also saw something more.

'At first she was her usual self,' he commented, 'almost a waxen figurine. But then all of a sudden she started to tell a joke, screwing up that perfect face in some cute but hilarious contortions.'

Carr spoke to Olivia about *Grease*, but she didn't really take him seriously; in the stage show, the lead female character Sandy was an all-American girl. Olivia, of course, had an Australian accent, but Carr said he could easily make Sandy an Australian student on a foreign exchange placement. The day after the dinner party, he arranged for the script to be delivered to Olivia, but she still had doubts it was the right project for her to get involved with.

'I was very reluctant,' she admitted, 'because *Toomorrow* was a bit of a disaster really. So I'd thought, I'm going to leave movies out and concentrate on my music ... also, I was concerned because I was twenty-nine and the role in *Grease* was for a seventeen year old.'

Olivia agreed she would consider doing *Grease*, but she insisted on a screen test with the leading man first. At this point, Olivia and John Travolta had never met, and he drove to her Malibu home for their first meeting. Even after the screen test, Olivia had doubts; she didn't feel it had gone especially well, but everyone else loved it – so, finally, she gave in and agreed to do the film.

The film version of *Grease*, often described as a 'musical romantic comedy', was directed by Randal Kleiser, and produced by Robert Stigwood & Allan Carr. In the film, Olivia and John Travolta played the parts of students Sandy Olsson and Danny Zuko, respectively. The cast also featured:

- Stockard Channing as Betty Rizzo
- Jeff Conaway as Kenickie
- Barry Pearl as Doody
- Didi Conn as Frenchy
- Michael Tucci as Sonny LaTierri
- Jamie Donnelly as Jan

- Kelly Ward as Roger 'Putzie'
- Dinah Manoff as Marty Maraschino
- Eve Arden as Principal McGee
- Dody Goodman as Blanche Hodel
- Sid Caesar as Coach Calhoun

The film premiered on 16th June 1978, and *Grease* went on to become the highest grossing film of the year. The film's budget was just $6 million, and it has taken around $395 at the box office alone.

Grease picked up four Golden Globe nominations and one Academy Award nomination, but it didn't win any of them. At the Oscars, John Farrar's *Hopelessly Devoted To You* was nominated in the Best Original Song category, but he lost out to Paul Jabara's *Last Dance*, which Donna Summer performed in *Thank God It's Friday*.

The accompanying soundtrack was a double album, and was released two months ahead of the film. The soundtrack yielded three of the biggest hits of Olivia's career, her solo *Hopelessly Devoted To You*, plus two of her three duets with John Travolta, *You're The One That I Want* and *Summer Nights*. The duo's third collaboration, *We Go Together*, wasn't released as a single. Olivia also contributed *Look At Me, I'm Sanda Dee (Reprise)* to the soundtrack.

The soundtrack yielded a further three hits: Frankie Valli's *Grease*, and *Sandy* and *Greased Lightnin'* by John Travolta.

GREASE was massively successful, and hit no.1 just about everywhere. In numerous countries, including Australia, Germany, the Netherlands, New Zealand, Norway, Spain, Sweden, Switzerland, the UK and the USA, the soundtrack topped the chart for 10+ weeks.

GREASE was the no.2 best-selling album of 1978, behind another soundtrack from a John Travolta film, *Saturday Night Fever*.

Deluxe Edition

To mark the 25th anniversary of *Grease*, the *GREASE* soundtrack was remastered and reissued in North America in 2003, and five years later the 30th anniversary of the film was celebrated in Europe. Both Deluxe Editions came with a bonus CD that featured the following tracks:

Grease (Instrumental Version)/Summer Nights (Sing-A-Long Version)/Hopelessly Devoted To You (Sing-A-Long Version)/You're The One That I Want (Sing-A-Long Version)/Sandy (Sing-A-Long Version)/Greased Lightnin' (Single Version)/Greased Up And Ready To Go (Instrumental)/The Grease Megamix/Grease – The Dream Mix/Summer Nights (Martian Remix)/You're The One That I Want (Martian Remix)

Estimates for how many copies *GREASE* how sold around the world vary wildly, from as little as 25 million to 40+ million. Whatever the true figure, there is no disputing *GREASE* is one of the best-selling soundtrack albums of all-time, and it may rank as high as no.3 in the all-time list, behind *SATURDAY NIGHT FEVER* and *THE BODYGUARD*.

15 ~ TOTALLY HOT

Please Don't Keep Me Waiting/Dancin' 'Round And 'Round/Talk To Me/Deeper Than The Night/Borrowed Time/A Little More Love/Never Enough/Totally Hot/Boats Against The Current/Gimme Some Lovin'

Produced by John Farrar.

Australia: Interfusion L36771 (1978).

20.11.78: peaked at no.**7**, charted for 23 weeks

UK: EMI EMA 789 (1978), EMAP 789 (picture disc, 1978).

9.12.78: 52-34-35-35-60-42-49-32-**30**-35-61-63-64-57

Canada
23.12.78: 98-79-79-51-45-39-36-22-18-11-6-**5**-**5**-6-7-11-12-15-14-18-18-18-18-17-18-18-26-29-36-73-85

Japan
5.11.78: peaked at no.**9**, charted for 18 weeks

Why not drive Olivia home tonight?
'Totally Hot'.
the latest cassette from
Olivia Newton John.

Netherlands
16.12.78: 14-9-6-7-6-**5-5-5**-13-22-26-35-37-43-48-x-x-47-44

New Zealand
21.01.79: 38-31-35-36-28-26-23-35-29-32-**18**

Norway
9.12.78: 16-14-13-7-5-5-5-5-**4-4-4**-5-5-8-8-10-11-17-17-20-20-20

Sweden
1.12.78: 10-**9**-11-**9**-10-14-23-25-44 (bi-weekly)

USA
9.12.78: 90-75-55-55-46-35-18-15-13-12-8-**7-7**-8-8-10-28-37-39-63-51-47-42-37-37-36-71-90

Olivia's first solo album, following the success of *Grease*, was eagerly anticipated and she didn't disappoint.

The album, *TOTALLY HOT*, was preceded by the single *A Little More Love*, which was a Top 10 hit in several countries. The album sleeve, with Olivia wearing black leather, mirrored the transformation her character Sandy made in *Grease*, and saw her image and music move from 'the girl next door' country star to a sexier image with a more aggressive, up-tempo sound.

Olivia wrote two of the tracks on *TOTALLY HOT* herself, *Borrowed Time* and *Talk To Me*, but neither was released as a single. Three singles were issued, with the first two – *A Little More Love* and *Deeper Than The Night* – enjoying chart success. The third single, the album's title cut, was less successful and failed to achieve Top 40 status anywhere, although the B-side *Dancin' 'Round And 'Round* did rise to no.29 on Billboard's country chart in the USA.

TOTALLY HOT was a Top 10 hit in numerous countries, peaking at no. 4 in Norway, no.5 in Canada and the Netherlands, no.7 in Australia and the USA, and no.9 in Japan and Sweden. The album was less successful in New Zealand and the UK, where it peaked at no.18 and no.30, respectively.

TOTALLY HOT was reissued in Japan in 2010, with two bonus tracks, an extended version of the title track and a live recording of *Love Is Alive*, which had appeared on Olivia's 1981 Japanese release, *LOVE PERFORMANCE*.

16 ~ XANADU

Magic ~ Olivia Newton-John
Suddenly ~ Olivia Newton-John with Cliff Richard
Dancin' ~ Olivia Newton-John with The Tubes
Suspended In Time ~ Olivia Newton-John
Whenever You're Away From Me ~ Olivia Newton-John with Gene Kelly
I'm Alive ~ Electric Light Orchestra
The Fall ~ Electric Light Orchestra
Don't Walk Away ~ Electric Light Orchestra
All Over The World ~ Electric Light Orchestra
Xanadu ~ Electric Light Orchestra & Olivia Newton-John

Produced by John Farrar.

Australia: Jet Records JT 6024 (1980).

28.07.80: peaked at no.**1** (6 weeks), charted for 31 weeks

UK: Jet Records JET LX 526 (1980).

19.07.80: 7-3-**2**-3-7-7-5-6-13-22-28-35-43-51-57-66-65

A Fantasy, A Musical, A Place Where Dreams Come True
XANADU
UNIVERSAL Presents A LAWRENCE GORDON Production
OLIVIA NEWTON-JOHN · GENE KELLY · "XANADU" · Also starring MICHAEL BECK
Written by RICHARD CHRISTIAN DANUS and MARC REID RUBEL Director of Photography VICTOR J. KEMPER, A.S.C.
Songs for OLIVIA NEWTON-JOHN by JOHN FARRAR Songs for ELECTRIC LIGHT ORCHESTRA by JEFF LYNNE
Musical Scoring by BARRY DeVORZON Executive Producer LEE KRAMER
Co-Producer JOEL SILVER Produced by LAWRENCE GORDON Directed by ROBERT GREENWALD
PG
DOLBY STEREO
ORIGINAL SOUNDTRACK ON MCA RECORDS AND TAPES
A UNIVERSAL PICTURE

Austria
1.08.80: 14-3-2-**1**-4-3-3-6-7-9-17-14 (bi-weekly)

Canada
19.07.80: 94-78-66-53-32-30-23-10-5-5-3-**2-2-2-2**-5-6-8-8-14-14-14-14-16-22-38-44

Germany
28.07.80: 20-4-2-2-2-2-2-**1**-3-3-3-3-4-4-7-6-9-9-9-13-11-19-24-27-23-41-36-41-58-58

Japan
16.07.80: peaked at no.**6**, charted for 45 weeks

Netherlands
26.07.80: 11-8-5-2-**1-1-1**-3-2-3-8-19-14-12-39-35-36-33-30-34-34-30-33

New Zealand
17.08.80: 37-21-12-11-13-9-**8**-9-12-13-16-19-20-30-35-x-x-50

Norway
5.07.80: 22-10-3-**1-1-1-1-1-1-1-1-1**-3-3-5-4-11-21-14-24-27-31-40-39-x-30-30-30-30-32-29-32-37

Spain
1.12.80: peaked at no.**1** (2 weeks), charted for 20 weeks

Sweden
25.07.80: 27-13-7-2-2-**1-1-1**-6-8-12-19-23-46 (bi-weekly)

Switzerland
1.08.80: 17-**1**-2-2-5-5-2-7-8-12-13 (bi-weekly)

USA
12.07.80: 79-71-57-44-26-20-18-17-12-10-8-7-**4-4-4**-6-10-12-16-42-41-53-57-62-62-62-60-58-58-83

Following the success of *Grease*, Olivia's management identified two films – both musicals – which they believed had the potential to further her acting career.

Allan Carr, who had worked with Olivia on *Grease*, wrote one of them, *Can't Stop The Music*. The script was very loosely based on the formation of, and the rise to fame of, the Village People, and would star members of the group as themselves. Carr also wrote a part for an actress who would play Samantha, a retired model who uses her connections to get the Village People their first recording contract – this was the part Carr envisaged Olivia playing.

However, in *Can't Stop The Music* the role of Samantha is almost peripheral, with the Village People taking centre stage. This is just one of the reasons Olivia eventually decided to go with the second offer on the table, *Xanadu*, which was billed as 'A Fantasy, A Musical, A Place Where Dreams Come True'.

Xanadu was written by Richard Christian Danus and Marc Reid Rubel, and directed by Robert Greenwald. The plot was loosely based on the 1947 film, *Down To Earth*, in which Rita Hayworth starred as Terpsichore, who in Greek mythology is one of the nine Muses, and the goddess of dance and chorus. In the film, Xanadu is a nightclub, which takes its name from the summer capital of Kublai Khan's Yuan Dynasty in China.

Olivia was cast in the lead female role, playing Kira, one of 'The Nine Sisters', nine beautiful and mysterious women who spring to life from a local mural. The cast also featured:

- Michael Beck as Sonny Malone.
- Gene Kelly as Danny McGuire.
- Matt Lattanzi as Danny McGuire (young).
- James Sloyan as Simpson.
- Dimitra Arliss as Helen.
- Katie Hanley as Sandra.
- Fred McCarren as Richie.
- Ren Woods as Jo.
- Melvin Jones as Big Al.
- Jo Ann Harris as a 1940s Singer.
- Ira Newborn as a 1940s Band Leader.

Xanadu's budget was $20 million, but unlike *Grease* it flopped badly at the box office, taking just $22.8 million. The accompanying soundtrack, however, was successful.

The soundtrack was split into two halves, with Olivia on side 1 and the Electric Light Orchestra (ELO) on side 2, with the title track – credited to Olivia & ELO – rounding off the album.

Three tracks featuring Olivia were released as singles, with the title track and *Magic* becoming major hits in numerous countries. *Suddenly*, a duet with Cliff Richard, was less successful, but still achieved Top 40 status in several countries.

Xanadu apart, three ELO singles were released from the soundtrack, *I'm Alive*, *All Over The World* and *Don't Walk Away*, and all three went Top 10 in one or more countries.

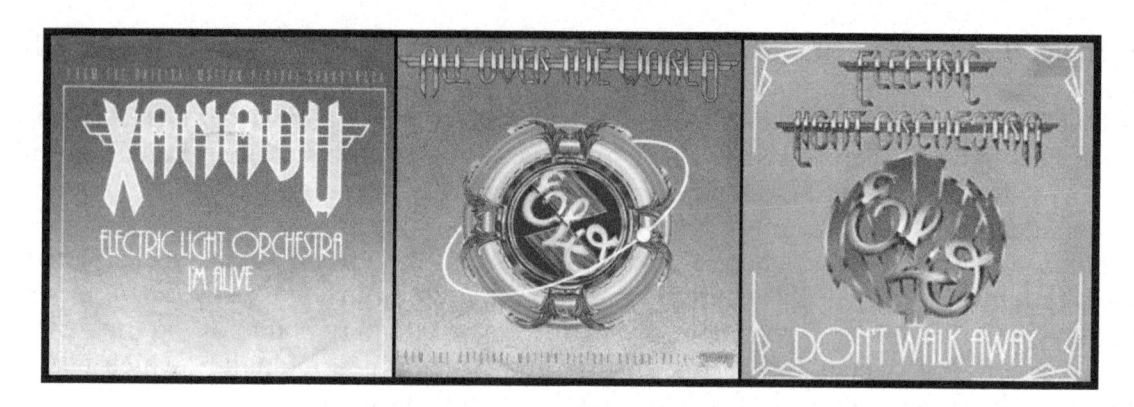

XANADU hit no.1 in Australia, Austria, Germany, Netherlands, Norway, Spain, Sweden and Switzerland, and charted at no.2 in Canada and the UK, no.4 in the USA, no.6 in Japan and no.8 in New Zealand.

Although the film *Xanadu* wasn't a hit, it did play a major role in Olivia's life, as she met her future husband Matt Lattanzi during filming. The couple married in 1984, and their daughter Chloe Rose was born in January 1986.

A double bill of *Xanadu* and *Can't Stop The Music*, the film Olivia turned down, was John J. B. Wilson's inspiration to start the Razzies. *Can't Stop The Music* has the dubious honour of being the first film to win the Worst Picture Golden Raspberry Award.

17 ~ PHYSICAL

Landslide/Stranger's Touch/Make A Move On Me/Falling/Love Make Me Strong/Physical/Silvery Rain/Carried Away/Recovery/The Promise (The Dolphin Song)

Produced by John Farrar.

Australia: Interfusion RML 53003 (1981).

12.10.81: peaked at no.**3**, charted for 39 weeks

UK: EMI EMC 3386 (1981).

31.10.81: 85-49-42-46-55-65-83-93
3.02.82: 37-**11**-15-14-24-33-51-45-50-75-81-62-89-90

Canada
7.11.81: 37-28-22-17-12-11-9-9-9-9-7-4-**3**-8-9-8-7-5-5-5-5-4-5-6-6-8-10-11-11-15-20-24-33-34
2.10.82: 60-67-78

Germany
23.11.81: 35-39-36-**30**-41-39-44-53-57-57-38-45-40-55-50-60-65-58-64

Japan
1.11.81: peaked at no.**5**, charted for 31 weeks

Netherlands
24.10.81: 45-13-**9**-15-17-23-21-25-35-37-x-31-x-39-35-40

New Zealand
30.08.81: 31-20-11-**8**-16-16-16-16-31-21-39-48
16.05.82: 34-32-44-45-50

Norway
14.11.81: 24-**8**-**8**-14-15-14-17-17-17-9-**8**-17-17-23-22-29-40

South Africa
31.07.82: peaked at no.**11**, charted for 9 weeks

Sweden
23.10.81: 11-4-**3**-7-13-21-36-30 (bi-weekly)

USA
31.10.81: 68-34-13-12-10-8-**6**-**6**-**6**-**6**-**6**-11-14-17-16-16-15-14-10-10-8-7-**6**-**6**-9-12-12-25-44-58-58-100

Olivia recorded her first solo studio album of the 1980s at the David J. Holman Studio in Los Angeles, in late 1980 and early 1981.

PHYSICAL, with its overtly sexual themes, proved hugely controversial – but hugely popular, too, with the title track topping Billboard's Hot 100 for ten straight weeks in the USA. For the first time, Olivia chose not to include any country songs on one of her albums, but she did record two songs with an ecological or animal rights theme, namely *Silvery Rain* and *The Promise (The Dolphin Song)*. The now iconic cover photograph was captured by renowned photographer Herb Ritts, during a photo shoot in Honolulu, Hawaii.

Interviewed by Billboard magazine, speaking about her move away from country music, Olivia acknowledged 'You might lose a few fans but you gain others. You have to do what's comfortable'. She went on to state 'I've gotten the confidence to be more adventurous whereas in the past I didn't think it was the time.'

Three singles were issued from *PHYSICAL*, with the title track preceding the album, and giving Olivia the biggest solo hit of her career in many countries. *Make A Move On Me* and *Landslide* followed, and both enjoyed Top 40 success in several countries.

As well as making numerous high profile TV appearances, Olivia promoted *PHYSICAL* with her fifth concert tour, which kicked off at the Merriweather Post Pavilion, Columbia, on 9th August 1982 and ran until mid-October the same year. Olivia also filmed a music video for every track on the album, in such locations as London, Honolulu and her Malibu home, with Brian Grant directing all ten promos. Her husband-to-be, Matt Lattanzi, featured in the *Landslide* music video.

A video compilation, also titled *Physical*, was released which brought together all the music videos, plus promos for *Magic*, *A Little More Love* and *Hopelessly Devoted To You*. Olivia picked up another Grammy for the compilation, for Video of the Year.

Olivia's Physical Tour was also released as a home video, variously titled *Olivia In Concert* or simply *Live!* – like the video compilation, it picked up a Grammy nomination, for Best Music Video, Long Form, but this time Olivia lost out to Duran Duran.

PHYSICAL achieved no.3 in Australia, Canada and Sweden, no.5 in Japan, no.6 in the USA, no.8 in New Zealand and Norway, no.9 in the Netherlands, no.11 in South Africa and the UK, and no.30 in Germany.

With global sales around the 10 million mark, *PHYSICAL* is generally acknowledged to be Olivia's best-selling solo album.

PHYSICAL was remastered and reissued in 2010, with two bonus tracks, *Heart Attack* and *Tied Up*.

18 ~ GREATEST HITS VOL.3 / VOL.2

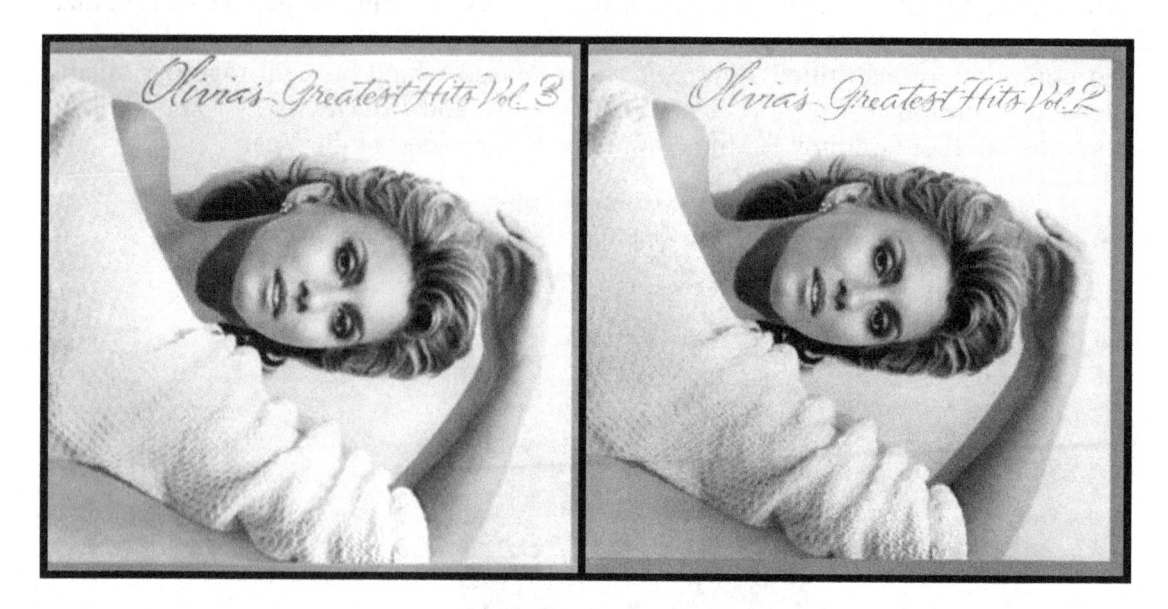

Australia: *Heart Attack/Magic/Physical/Deeper Than The Night/Hopelessly Devoted To You/Make A Move On Me/Landslide/A Little More Love/You're The One That I Want/Tied Up/Suddenly/Totally Hot/The Promise/Xanadu*

Europe/Japan/USA: *Heart Attack/Magic/Physical/Hopelessly Devoted To You/Make A Move On Me/A Little More Love/You're The One That I Want/Tied Up/Suddenly/Xanadu*

Australia: Interfusion RML 52015 (1982).

15.11.82: peaked at no.**1** (2 weeks), charted for 38 weeks

UK: Not Released.

Canada
2.11.82: 77-60-38-29-22-15-10-8-8-7-**6-6**-11-11-11-24-21-20-19-18-19-19-22-38-37-34-31-37-44-53-63-63-61-57-53-51-51-47-46-46-45-46-50-50-47-45-45-46-46-45-42-41-39-39-39-45-47-51-49-47-45-42-42-42-42-42-43-41-41-42-42-46-50

Germany
15.11.82: 45-53-54-**33**-54

Japan
21.10.82: peaked at no.**12**, charted for 22 weeks

New Zealand
28.11.82: 8-9-**3**-4-4-4-4-4-8-19-29-38-49
3.04.83: 23-22-30-50-34-30

South Africa
4.12.82: peaked at no.**4**, charted for 13 weeks

USA: MCA MCA-5347 (1982).

9.10.82: 41-27-21-18-18-**16-16-16-16**-34-33-33-33-35-35-36-43-43-42-40-40-39-39-56-
 56-86-84-81-75-66-62-50-45-41-39-36-48-51-63-67-80-76-73-78-75-71-78-75-71-77-
 89-89-87-85-90-88-99-93-90-92-88-91-80-79-79-77-67-70-78-77-73-84-83-88-87-99

Olivia's second major international hits compilation was titled *GREATEST HITS VOL.2* in most countries, but given a similarly titled album had already been released in Australasia, it was titled *GREATEST HITS VOL.3* there.

The compilation featured two new songs, *Heart Attack* and *Tied Up*, and both were released as singles. Both achieved Top 40 status, but *Heart Attack* was far more successful than *Tied Up*.

Four tracks – *Deeper Than The Night*, *Landslide*, *Totally Hot* and *The Promise* – were omitted from the compilation released in Europe, Japan and the USA, compared with the Australian version.

The album went all the way to no.1 in Australia, and charted at no.3 in New Zealand, no.4 in South Africa, no.6 in Canada, no.12 in Japan, no.16 in the USA and no.33 in Germany.

In some countries, including the Netherlands and the UK, a greatest hits package with a different track listing and sleeve design was released instead of *GREATEST HITS Vol.2 / VOL.3*.

19 ~ OLIVIA'S GREATEST HITS / *20 GROOTSTE HITS*

Physical/Tied Up/Heart Attack/Make A Move On Me/You're The One That I Want/ What Is Life/Xanadu/Summer Nights/Landslide/Take Me Home Country Roads/A Little More Love/Magic/Suddenly/Changes/Hopelessly Devoted To You/Sam/If Not For You/Banks Of The Ohio/Rosewater/I Honestly Love You

Australia: Not Released.

UK: EMI EMTV 36 (1982).

23.10.82: 38-11-9-15-24-23-23-30-30-37-37-15-**8-8**-10-12-20-28-37-30-31-39-46-47-68-79-87-71-70-71-x-93
17.09.83: 47-x-81-93
19.11.83: 83
28.01.84: 72-92-77

Netherlands
13.11.82: 21-17-25-**12**-24-19-26-32-43

Whereas *GREATEST HITS VOL.2 / VOL.3* focused on singles Olivia had released since her previous greatest hits package in 1977, a completely different compilation was issued in the UK and the Netherlands, which included a selection of earlier recordings as well.
  OLIVIA'S GREATEST HITS charted at no.8 in the UK and no.12 in the Netherlands.

20 ~ TWO OF A KIND

Twist Of Fate ~ Olivia Newton-John
Take A Chance ~ Olivia Newton-John & John Travolta
It's Gonna Be Special ~ Patti Austin
Catch 22 (2 Steps Forward, 3 Steps Back) ~ Steve Kipner
Shaking You ~ Olivia Newton-John
Livin' In Desperate Times ~ Olivia Newton-John
The Perfect One ~ Boz Skaggs
Ask The Lonely ~ Journey
Prima Donna ~ Chicago (2)
Night Music ~ David Foster

UK Bonus Track: 'Introductions by John Travolta & Olivia Newton-John'.

USA Bonus Tracks: *Heart Attack*, *Tied Up* – Olivia Newton-John.

Produced by David Foster, except *It's Gonna Be Special* by Quincy Jones, *Catch 22 (2 Steps Forward, 3 Steps Back)* by Humberto Gatica & Steve Kipner, *The Perfect One* by David Paich & Steve Porcaro and *Ask The Lonely* by Mike Stone.

Australia: Interfusion RML 53110 (1983).

19.12.83: peaked at no.**33**, charted for 24 weeks

JOHN TRAVOLTA OLIVIA NEWTON-JOHN
It took a
Twist of Fate
to make them
two of a kind.
Two of a Kind
TWENTIETH CENTURY-FOX PRESENTS
A JOE WIZAN-ROGER M. ROTHSTEIN PRODUCTION OF A JOHN HERZFELD FILM
JOHN TRAVOLTA OLIVIA NEWTON-JOHN TWO OF A KIND OLIVER REED
BEATRICE STRAIGHT SCATMAN CROTHERS AND CHARLES DURNING AS CHARLIE
DIRECTOR OF PHOTOGRAPHY FRED KOENEKAMP, A.S.C. MUSIC ADAPTED BY PATRICK WILLIAMS
PRODUCED BY ROGER M. ROTHSTEIN AND JOE WIZAN WRITTEN AND DIRECTED BY JOHN HERZFELD
20th CENTURY FOX
ORIGINAL SOUNDTRACK RECORDING AVAILABLE ON MCA RECORDS AND TAPES
DISTRIBUTED BY TWENTIETH CENTURY-FOX FILM ASSOCIATES
COPYRIGHT ©1983 TWENTIETH CENTURY-FOX

UK: EMI EMC 1654611 (1983).

TWO OF A KIND wasn't a hit in the UK.

Canada
26.11.83: 84-60-49-36-36-34-34-31-**30**-32-32-33-34-39-45-45-47-57-65-76-79

Japan
16.12.83: peaked at no.**29**, charted for 21 weeks

USA
10.12.83: 72-43-30-30-29-28-27-27-**26**-36-41-45-56-58-79

Originally titled *Second Chance*, *Two Of A Kind* was the second film Olivia made with John Travolta, but it was nowhere near as successful as the first, *Grease*.

A romantic/fantasy comedy, *Two Of A Kind* was written and directed by John Herzfeld. It was filmed on location in New York City, and at three California studios, namely MGM Studios in Culver City, 20th Century Fox Studios in Century City and The Burbank Studios in Burbank.

In *Two Of A Kind* Olivia played Debbie Wylder, a bank teller who a cash-strapped inventor Zack Melon – played by John Travolta – attempts to rob. The cast also included:

- Oliver Reed as Beasley.
- Charles Durning as Charlie.
- Beatrice Straight as Ruth.
- Scatman Crothers as Earl.
- Richard Bright as Stuart.
- Toni Kalem as Terri.
- Ernie Hudson as Detective Skaggs.
- Gene Hackman as God.

Like *Xanadu*, *Two Of A Kind* flopped at the box office, taking just $23.6 million, but like *Xanadu* the accompanying soundtrack was more successful.

Olivia featured on four of the ten tracks on the soundtrack, including *Take A Chance*, another duet with John Travolta. Two tracks, *Twist Of Fate* and *Livin' In Desperate Times*, were released as singles and achieved Top 40 status.

TWO OF A KIND charted at no.26 in the USA, no.29 in Japan, no.30 in Canada and no.33 in Australia, but it wasn't a hit in the UK.

21 ~ SOUL KISS

Toughen Up/Soul Kiss/Queen Of The Publication/Emotional Tangle/Culture Shock/Moth To A Flame/Overnight Observation/You Were Great, How Was I?/Driving Music/The Right Moment

Europe (excluding UK) & Japan Bonus Track: *Electric* (after *Driving Music*).

Produced by John Farrar.

Australia: Interfusion RML 53127 (1985).

25.11.85: peaked at no.**19**, charted for 14 weeks

UK: Mercury MERH 77 (1985).

8.03.86: **66**-90-98

Canada
19.10.85: 82-71-51-38-36-**34-34**-40-42-52-55-55-55-59-68-79

Germany
11.11.85: 56-**54**-59

Japan
21.10.85: peaked at no.**5**, charted for 7 weeks

Netherlands
2.11.85: **36**-46-55-58

New Zealand
15.12.85: **43**

Sweden
15.11.85: **46** (bi-weekly)

USA
2.11.85: 60-41-31-**29-29-29**-34-54-65-65-87-97

Following the success of *PHYSICAL*, Olivia's follow-up *SOUL KISS* generally disappointed, and didn't sell or chart nearly as well.

In addition to TV appearances, Olivia promoted the album with five music videos, for *Toughen Up, Emotional Tangle, Culture Shock, Soul Kiss* and *The Right Moment*, which were released as a home video compilation.

In most countries, *Soul Kiss* and *Toughen Up*, a song offered to and rejected by Tina Turner, were released as singles. The former enjoyed reasonable success, but *Toughen Up* – which wasn't issued in the UK – was only a minor hit in Australia and missed the charts in most countries.

SOUL KISS achieved no.5 in Japan, no.19 in Australia, no.29 in the USA, no.34 in Canada, no.36 in the Netherlands, no.43 in New Zealand and no.46 in Sweden, but peaked outside the Top 50 in Germany and the UK.

22 ~ THE RUMOUR

The Rumour/Love And Let Live/Can't We Talk It Over In Bed/Let's Talk About Tomorrow/ It's Not Heaven/Get Out/Big And Strong/Car Games/Walk Through The Fire/Tutta La Vita

Australia Bonus Track: *It's Always Australia For Me* (after *It's Not Heaven*).

Produced by Davitt Sigerson, except *The Rumour* by Elton John & James Newton Howard and *Can't We Talk It Over In Bed* by Hank Medress & Sandy Linzer.

Australia: Interfusion TVL 93263 (1988).

25.09.88: 43-32-41-**30**-44

UK: Mercury 834 957-1 (1988).

THE RUMOUR wasn't a hit in the UK.

Canada
24.09.88: **97**

Japan
25.08.88: peaked at no.**31**, charted for 8 weeks

Netherlands
24.09.88: **96**

USA
3.09.88: 89-73-**67-67**-79

THE RUMOUR was the first album Olivia released, which wasn't produced by her long-time collaborator, John Farrar.

The album failed to reverse Olivia's declining sales, despite the involvement of Elton John, who co-wrote the title track with Bernie Taupin, as well as playing piano and singing backing on the recording. Olivia showcased the songs on the album with an hour long home video, *Olivia Down Under*, which saw her performing songs from the album set against a spectacular Australian backdrop.

Released as the lead single, *The Rumour* achieved Top 40 status, but only just. The follow-up, the provocatively titled *Can't We Talk It Over In Bed*, was only released in Australia and North America, but it wasn't a hit.

It's Always Australia For Me, which was only released on the Australian issue of *THE RUMOUR*, was released as a limited edition single in Australia, to mark the country's bicentenary, but it wasn't a hit.

THE RUMOUR achieved no.30 in Australia and no.31 in Japan, but peaked well outside the Top 40 in Canada, the Netherlands and the USA, and failed to chart in most countries, including the UK.

23 ~ BACK TO BASICS – THE ESSENTIAL COLLECTION 1971-1992

Australia: *I Need Love/Deeper Than A River/Not Gonna Be The One/I Want To Be Wanted/If Not For You/Banks Of The Ohio/Let Me Be There/I Honestly Love You/If You Love Me (Let Me Know)/Have You Never Been Mellow/Don't Stop Believin'/Sam/A Little More Love/Physical/Make A Move On Me/Hopelessly Devoted To You/Xanadu/Magic/Twist Of Fate/Soul Kiss/The Grease Megamix*

UK: *If Not For You/Banks Of The Ohio/Take Me Home Country Roads/I Honestly Love You/Have You Never Been Mellow/Sam/You're The One That I Want/Hopelessly Devoted To You/Summer Nights/A Little More Love/Xanadu/Suddenly/Physical/I Need Love/Not Gonna Be The One/I Want To Be Wanted/Deeper Than A River*

Australia: Festival Records TVD 93361 (1992).

30.08.92: 37-25-**15-15**-20-24-27-37-43
1.03.98: 33-30-25-29
21.04.03: 51-33-28-21-59-67 *(THE SINGLES COLLECTION)*

UK: Mercury 512641-1 (1992).

25.07.92: **12**-20-21-34-55-71

New Zealand
4.10.92: **7**-8-8-12-16-26-31-49

29.03.98: 43-42 *(THE SINGLES COLLECTION)*

This compilation, with a varied track listing chosen to reflect Olivia's successful singles in different countries, also included four new recordings: *Deeper Than A River*, *I Need Love*, *I Want To Be Wanted* and *Not Gonna Be The One*.

Olivia planned to promote *BACK TO BASICS* with her first American tour in a decade, with the opening night scheduled for 6th August 1992 at Caesar's Palace, Las Vegas. Over the 4th of July weekend, she took a break from rehearsals, to relax with her husband Matt Lattanzi, and good friends John & Pat Farrar, at one of her favourite holiday retreats, the San Juan archipelago. It was here that Matt took a phone call, with two important messages: Olivia's father, who was battling liver cancer, had died, and Olivia's doctor needed to see her urgently.

Not sure how his wife would cope with two pieces of bad news, Matt told Olivia of her father's passing, but delayed letting her know her doctor needed to see her until after the weekend. When she contacted her doctor, Olivia was devastated to learn she had been diagnosed with breast cancer.

The planned tour was cancelled, and on 14th July Olivia released an official statement, revealing she had breast cancer. It was, she admits, 'a very, very difficult time'. The diagnosis meant she had no real time to grieve for her father, and she was denied the chance to attend the funeral, as she had to see doctors, and undergo surgery and chemotherapy.

As a result of her battle against breast cancer, which she eventually won, Olivia was unable to promote *BACK TO BASICS* as she had planned, and consequently the album wasn't as successful as it might otherwise have been. Nevertheless, it achieved no.7 in New Zealand, no.12 in the UK and no.15 in Australia.

In the USA, where the compilation peaked at a lowly no.121 on the Billboard 200, the track listing was as follows:

Deeper Than A River/Not Gonna Be The One/I Want To Be Wanted/I Need Love/ Twist Of Fate/Physical/Magic/Deeper Than The Night/A Little More Love/You're The One That I Want/Summer Nights/Hopelessly Devoted To You/Sam/Please Mr. Please/Have You Never Been Mellow/If You Love Me(Let Me Know)/Let Me Be There/I Honestly Love You

One of the new songs, *I Need Love*, was released as the lead single from the compilation. It was a minor hit in Australia, the UK and the USA, but failed to chart in most countries. The follow-up, *Deeper Than A River*, was only released in Australia and North America – it failed to chart on any mainstream charts, although it was a Top 20 Adult Contemporary hit in Canada and the USA.

Limited Tour Edition

In 1998, *BACK TO BASICS* was reissued in Australia as *'THE SINGLES COLLECTION – LIMITED TOUR EDITION'* (Festival Records D 93361). The original track listing was unchanged, however, the reissue came with a bonus CD that featured:

No Matter What You Do/Don't Cut Me Down/It's Always Australia For Me/Can't We Talk It Over In Bed/The Rumour/Please Mr. Please/Jolene/Don't Cry For Me Argentina/Heart Attack/Toughen Up

THE SINGLES COLLECTION – LIMITED TOUR EDITION charted at no.21 in Australia and no.42 in New Zealand.

24 ~ GAIA – ONE WOMAN'S JOURNEY

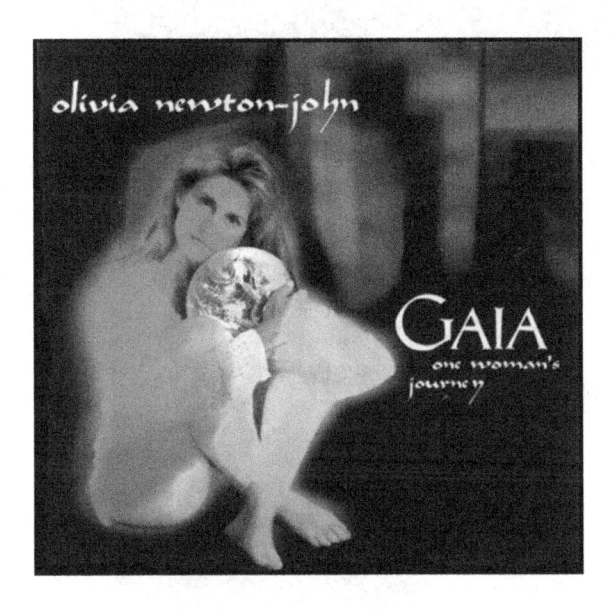

Trust Yourself/No Matter What You Do/No Other Love/Pegasus/Why Me/Don't Cut Me Down/Gaia/Do You Feel/I Never Knew Love/Silent Ruin/Not Gonna Give In To It/The Way Of Love

Produced by Colin Bayley, Murray Burns & Olivia Newton John.

Australia: Festival Records TVD 93406 (1994).

2.10.94: **7**-9-18-28-40-44-x-x-x-x-41

UK: D Sharp DSH LCD 7017 (1994).

4.02.95: 37-**33**-43-67

In Olivia's own words: '*GAIA* was born out of my decision to write, record & co-produce, for the first time, an album of songs about my personal feelings.'

Those personal feelings, of course, were massively influenced by Olivia's fight against breast cancer and her father's passing. In the liner notes, she cited her inspiration for each song, and revealed where and when each song was written. These include:

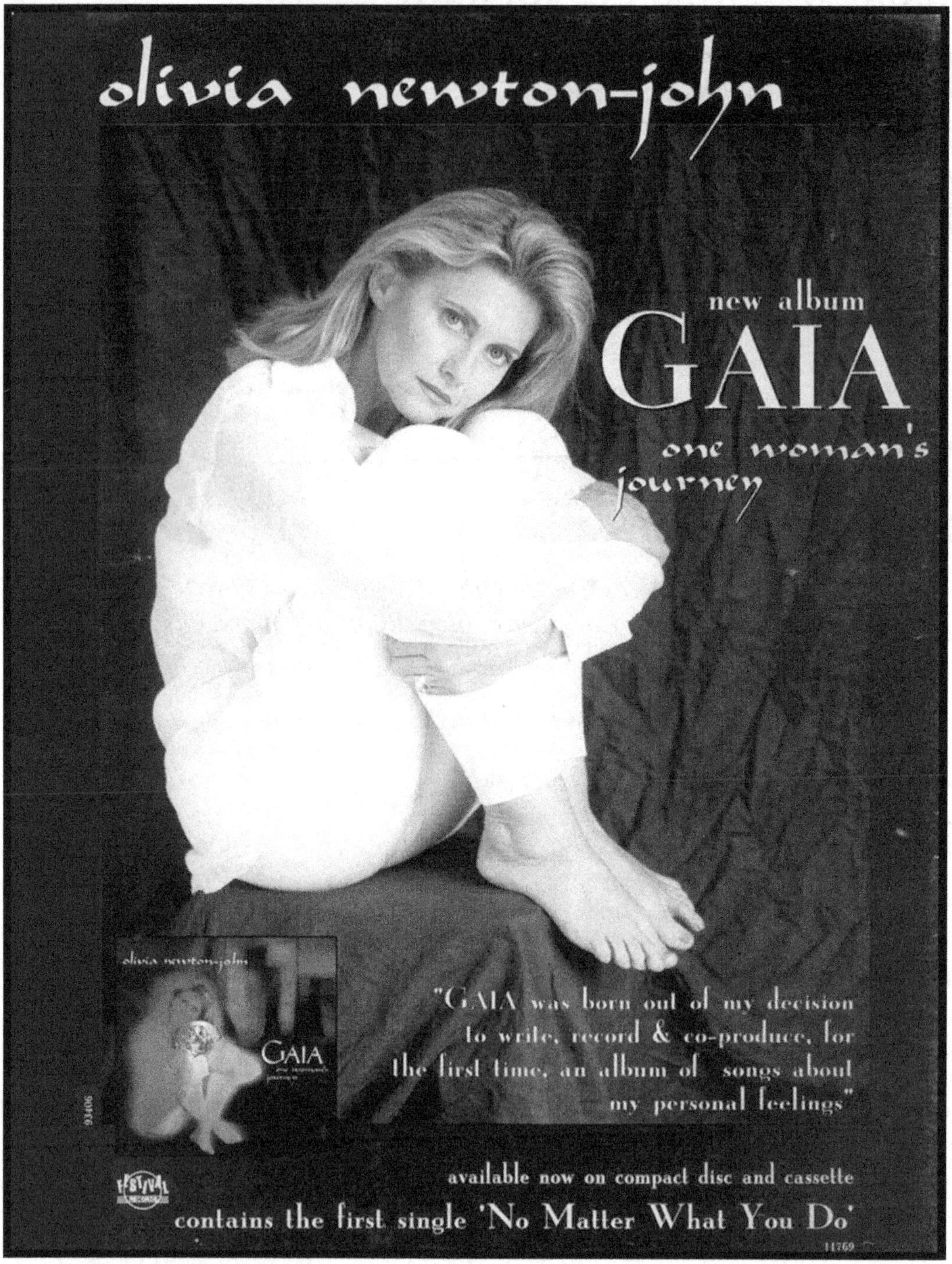
olivia newton-john
new album
GAIA
one woman's journey
olivia newton-john
GAIA
"GAIA was born out of my decision
to write, record & co-produce, for
the first time, an album of songs about
my personal feelings"
available now on compact disc and cassette
contains the first single 'No Matter What You Do'

- *Gaia*: 'Gaia (pronounced Guy-ya) is the spirit of Mother Earth. She is the giver of dreams and the nourisher of plants and young children. The song came to me at 3.00 AM on a cold winter morning in Byron Bay and I was compelled to write and finish it. I feel the spirit of Mother Earth spoke to me. August 1993.'

- *Not Gonna Give In To It*: 'I wrote this after chemotherapy treatment. It speaks for itself. Los Angeles, 1992.'

- *Why Me*: 'I wrote this song the night after my surgery, as I was pondering the question "why me" as everyone does. My father died with dignity of cancer on the day I was diagnosed and he never complained for a moment. This is for him. Los Angeles, August 1992.'

- *No Matter What You Do*: 'This song came to me in the car on the way to the studio. It was during a time when I was having a lot of problems and I sent this song to all the negative forces in my life. December 1993.'

- *No Other Love*: 'For the loves of my life, Matt and Chloe. Byron Bay, January 1994.'

In Australia, Olivia was still contracted to Festival Records, so *GAIA* was released as normal, but in other countries the album was released on various small, independent labels.

GAIA charted at no.7 in Australia and no.33 in the UK, but surprisingly it wasn't a hit in most countries.

GAIA was recorded in Australia, but Olivia chose to record her follow-up in Nashville, Tennessee, and 1998's *BACK WITH A HEART* saw her returning to country music. The album was a minor no.59 hit in the USA, but it failed to achieve Top 40 status anywhere.

25 ~ HIGHLIGHTS FROM THE MAIN EVENT

John, Olivia & Anthony: *Overture/Age Of Reason/Phantom Of The Opera/A Little More Love/Age Of Reason*
Anthony: *This Is The Moment*
Olivia: *Hopelessly Devoted To You*
John: *Every Time You Cry*
John & Olivia: *Please Don't Ask Me/You're The One That I Want*
Olivia & Anthony: *The Long And Winding Road/Take Me Home Country Roads/I Honestly Love You/Love Is A Gift*
John & Anthony: *That's Life/Bad Habits/Granada*
John, Olivia & Anthony: *You've Lost That Loving Feeling/Summer Nights/If Not For You/Let Me Be There/Raindrops Keep Falling On My Head/Jolene/Hearts On Fire/Don't You Know It's Magic/You're The Voice*

Produced by Glenn Wheatley.

Australia: BMG Australia/RCA 74321638832 (1998), 74321864872 (Limited Edition, 2001).

6.12.98: 3-2-**1-1**-2-6-6-10-13-17-16-24-31-24-42-x-18-7-10-20-33-32-31-7-32-40-44-42-x-44

UK: Not Released.

JOHN
FARNHAM
OLIVIA
NEWTON-JOHN
ANTHONY
WARLOW
THE
MAIN
EVENT
G
FOR GENERAL
EXHIBITION

The Main Event Tour, which kicked off in Melbourne, Australia, in October 1998, featured Olivia, John Farnham and Anthony Warlow.

Olivia, John and Anthony played 11 dates at six different Australian venues:

- 28th October: Melbourne Park, Melbourne.
- 6th & 7th November: Derwent Entertainment Centre, Hobart.
- 16th & 17th November: Sydney Entertainment Centre, Sydney.
- 25th November: Brisbane Entertainment Centre, Brisbane.
- 2nd & 3rd December: Adelaide Entertainment Centre, Adelaide.
- 11th December: Burswood Dome, Burswood.
- 17th December: Sydney Entertainment Centre, Sydney.
- 19th December: Brisbane Entertainment Centre, Brisbane.

A live album, *HIGHLIGHTS FROM THE MAIN EVENT*, plus a home video titled *The Main Event*, were released in Australia only, even before the last few concerts had been staged, and proved hugely successful.

The album made its chart debut at no.3, and hit no.1 two weeks later, topping the chart for two weeks over the busy festive period. The following year, the album picked up a 5 x Platinum award, denoting sales of 350,000.

HIGHLIGHTS FROM THE MAIN EVENT was reissued in 2001, with three bonus tracks:

- John & Olivia: *Two Strong Hearts*
- Olivia & Anthony: *Not Gonna Give In To It*
- John & Anthony: *Help*

26 ~ THE DEFINITIVE COLLECTION

You're The One That I Want/Xanadu/Magic/Sam/I Honestly Love You/Hopelessly Devoted To You/Suddenly/I Need Love/A Little More Love/Summer Nights/Physical/What Is Life/Heart Attack/Landslide/Make A Move On Me/Have You Never Been Mellow/Deeper Than The Night/Banks Of The Ohio/Take Me Home Country Roads/Long Live Love/If Not For You/The Grease Megamix

Australia: Not Released.

UK: Universal 584 279-2 (2002).

30.10.04: **11**-17-23-32-39-47-51-59-57-59
23.04.05: 92-68-97

Japan
21.04.03: peaked at no.**13**, charted for 20 weeks

Norway
20.07.02: 29-20-**18**-35

This compilation, which surprisingly wasn't released in Australia or North America, brought together 22 of Olivia's biggest hits.
 The album charted at no.11 in the UK and no.18 in Norway, but failed to chart in most countries where it was released.

In Japan, the compilation wasn't released until 2003, and *Jolene* replaced *Make A Move On Me*. The running order of the tracks was also completely different on the Japanese release:

Have You Never Been Mellow/Xanadu/Physical/I Honestly Love You/Jolene/Magic/You're The One That I Want/Sam/Take Me Home Country Roads/If Not For You/Hopelessly Devoted To You/Suddenly/I Need Love/Summer Nights/Heart Attack/Landslide/A Little More Love/What Is Life/Deeper Than The Night/Banks Of The Ohio/Long Live Love/The Grease Megamix

THE DEFINITIVE COLLECTION achieved no.13 in Japan.

27 ~ (2)

Sunburned Country ~ Olivia & Keith Urban
Lift Me Up ~ Olivia & Darren Hayes
I'll Come Runnin' ~ Olivia & Tina Arena
Tenterfield Saddler ~ Olivia & Peter Allen
I Will Be Right Here ~ Olivia & David Campbell
I Love You Crazy ~ Olivia & Human Nature
Bad About You ~ Olivia & Billy Thorpe
I'm Counting On You ~ Olivia & Johnny O'Keefe
Never Far Away ~ Olivia & Richard Marx
Happy Day ~ Olivia & Jimmy Little
Act Of Faith ~ Olivia & Michael McDonald
Physical (Acoustic Version) ~ Olivia

Japan only: *Let It Be Me* ~ Cliff Richard & *Physical (Samba Version)* (replacing *Physical (Acoustic Version)*)

Produced by Charles Fisher.

Australia: Festival Mushroom Records 336022 (2002).

17.11.02: **5**-11-15-16-19-17-18-31-60-64-86
21.04.03: 89-66-46

Olivia Newton-John (2)

Olivia returns with her finest album yet.... featuring duet performances with some of Australia's premier international acts as well as some honorary 'ozzie' guests.

David Campbell
Darren Hayes
Tina Arena
Human Nature
Keith Urban
Johnny O'Keefe
Richard Marx
Billy Thorpe
Michael McDonald
Jimmy Little

Plus

The beautiful 'new recording' of Tenterfield Saddler featuring **Olivia** and **Peter Allen**

UK: Not Released.

'This album,' Olivia wrote on the album's liner notes, 'is a labour of love. I have always wanted to record a CD of duets with all those talented Australians ... with a couple of my American friends as a bonus – honorary Ozzies for this album!'.

Olivia's duet partners on *(2)* included Americans Michael McDonald and Richard Marx, and Australians Darren Hayes, Keith Urban, Tina Arena and Human Nature. The album, which was recorded in less than three months, closed with an acoustic version of Olivia's hit, *Physical*. Olivia dedicated the album to her mother, Irene.

Most of the duets were newly recorded, however, *Tenderfield Saddler* with Peter Allen and *I'm Counting On You* with Johnny O'Keefe featured archive recordings, with Olivia adding new vocals. *Tenterfield Saddler* was released as a promotional only CD single, but it wasn't given a full release and wasn't a hit.

One planned duet – *True To Yourself* with Vanessa Amorosi – had to be dropped from the album's track listing due to contractual reasons.

Initially, *(2)* was only released in Australia, where it made its chart debut at its peak position, no.5. However, two years later the album was released in Japan, with one bonus track, Olivia's duet with Cliff Richard, *Let It Be Me*. The Japanese release also saw the samba version of *Physical* replacing the acoustic version.

Olivia released a second duets album, *A CELEBRATION IN SONG*, in 2008 but it wasn't a hit anywhere.

28 ~ INDIGO – WOMEN OF SONG

How Insensitive/Love Me Or Leave Me/Cry Me A River/Anyone Who Had A Heart/Where Have All The Flowers Gone/How Glad I Am/Lovin' You/Rainy Days And Mondays/Send In The Clowns/Summertime/Alfie

Produced by Phil Ramone.

Australia: Festival Records D 338345 (2004).

31.10.04: **15**-17-25-38-69-49-39-44-49-62

UK: Universal 987 090-6 (2005).

23.04.05: **27**-54-92

This album, as the sub-title 'Women of Song' suggests, saw Olivia paying tribute to some of the female artists she admired and respected, for whatever reason. In the liner notes, Olivia identified the artist she was paying tribute to, and why. These are the artists she cited:

- *How Insensitive* – Astrud Gilberto.
- *Love Me Or Leave Me* – Doris Day.
- *Cry Me A River* – Julie London.

La Fnac présente
le nouvel album de OLIVIA
NEWTON-JOHN
LE PRIX VERT
fnac
indigo
Women Of Songs
Album Produit par
PHIL RAMONE.
Hommage à 11 grandes
chanteuses qui ont inspirées
sa carrière ;
Minnie Ripperton
Dionne Warwick
Cilla Black
Astrud Gilberto
Joan Baez
Judy Collins
Julie London
Karen Carpenter
Doris Day
Nina Simone
Nancy Wilson
olivia
newton-john
indigo
fnac
.com

- *Anyone Who Had A Heart* – Cilla Black.
- *Where Have All The Flowers Gone* – Joan Baez.
- *How Glad I Am* – Nancy Wilson.
- *Lovin' You* – Minnie Riperton.
- *Rainy Days And Mondays* – Karen Carpenter.
- *Send In The Clowns* – Judy Collins & Barbra Streisand.
- *Summertime* – Nina Simone.
- *Alfie* – Dionne Warwick.

Olivia also explained why she chose each particular song, for example:

- *Anyone Who Had A Heart*: 'I sang this song in the finals of a talent contest on an Australian TV show called *Sing, Sing, Sing* in 1964. I won, so this song is very important to me because the prize was a trip by ship to London which I took in 1966.'

- *Lovin' You*: 'Minnie was the first woman that I knew who died of breast cancer. I remember playing tennis at a celebrity tournament in the mid 70's with Helen Reddy, Linda Ronstadt and Minnie. Not only was she a remarkable songwriter and singer with an incredible range, but a brave and inspirational woman.'

- *Rainy Days And Mondays*: 'Karen was my friend. She had one of the most beautiful, rich and emotional voices that I have ever heard. I was very nervous to sing this, for who can follow Karen – but knowing her, I think she would forgive me!'

Recorded at the Indigo Ranch Studios in Malibu, California, *INDIGO – WOMEN OF SONG* charted at no.15 in Australia and no.27 in the UK, but failed to chart in most countries.

29 ~ STRONGER THAN BEFORE

Stronger Than Before/When You Believe/Phenomenal Woman/Under The Skin/Pass It On/ That's All I Know For Sure/When I Needed You/Can I Trust Your Arms/Don't Stop Believin' (Bossa Nova Version)/Serenity

Australia: ONJ Productions 510112891-2 (2005).

19.03.06: 87-72-x-**39**-47-88

UK: Not Released.

The story of this album, Olivia explains in her liner notes, started more than 13 years ago when, whilst out to lunch with her mother just after she'd completed her breast cancer treatments, Olivia met a woman who recognised her in the ladies' room – a woman who told her 'I had breast cancer twenty years ago and I'm fine'.

That moment, Olivia says, made a huge difference to her. 'By way of this CD,' she added, 'I am grateful to be able to pass on that torch with these songs of inspiration, encouragement and understanding to all those facing breast cancer or any other challenging journey.'

Olivia co-wrote four of the songs on STRONGER THAN BEFORE, the title track, *Under The Skin, That's All I Know For Sure* and *Can I Trust Your Arms*. She wrote *That's All I Know For Sure* for her daughter Chloe, who repaid the compliment by gifting the words to *Can I Trust Your Arms* to Olivia, as a Christmas gift. 'I wrote the melody for it, alone at the piano,' said Olivia, 'and that's how we've recorded it, keeping it very simple and personal.'

30 ~ THIS CHRISTMAS

Baby It's Cold Outside/Rockin' Around The Christmas Tree/I'll Be Home For Christmas/This Christmas/Silent Night/The Christmas Waltz/Have Yourself A Merry Little Christmas/Winter Wonderland/White Christmas/I Think you Might Like It/The Christmas Song/Deck The Halls/Auld Lang Syne – Christmas Time Is Here (Medley)

Produced by Randy Waldman.

Australia: Universal 060253717455 (2012).

2.12.12: 99-x-43-**33**-41-61

UK: Universal 060253717455 (2012).

THIS CHRISTMAS wasn't a hit in the UK.

USA
1.12.12: **81**-x-x-86

Although they remained good friends, Olivia hadn't worked with John Travolta since the 1983 film, *Two Of A Kind*.
   The idea of recording an album together was born when Olivia sent John Travolta a Christmas card, in which she noted *You're The One That I Want* from *Grease* had become the best-selling duet in pop music history.

'I thought to myself, wouldn't people want to hear us do other songs?' said Travolta, 'and immediately came up with the idea of doing a holiday album together ... from the moment we decided to do this, magic happened.'

Amazingly, all the songs on the album were recorded in one take, and all were duets, except *The Christmas Waltz*, which credited John Travolta only. *Rockin' Around The Christmas Tree* featured Kenny G, *I'll Be Home For Christmas* featured Barbra Streisand, *This Christmas* featured Chick Corea, *Have Yourself A Merry Little Christmas* featured Cliff Richard, *Winter Wonderland* featured Tony Bennett & Count Basie Orchestra and *Deck The Halls* featured James Taylor.

Olivia and John Travolta made several TV appearances together, to promote the album, and although no singles were released they did film a music video for the one new song on the album, *I Think You Might Like It*.

THIS CHRISTMAS charted at no.33 in Australia, and was a minor hit in the USA, but in common with Olivia's recent albums it failed to chart in most countries.

Olivia and John Travolta agreed to donate their artist royalties from *THIS CHRISTMAS* to their respective charities, Olivia's Cancer and Wellness Centre and John's Jett Travolta Foundation for children with disabilities.

THIS CHRISTMAS was the fourth festive album Olivia released, following *'TIS THE SEASON* (which she recorded with Vince Gill) in 2000, *THE CHRISTMAS COLLECTION* in 2001 and *CHRISTMAS WISH* in 2007.

31 ~ HIGHLIGHTS FROM TWO STRONG HEARTS LIVE

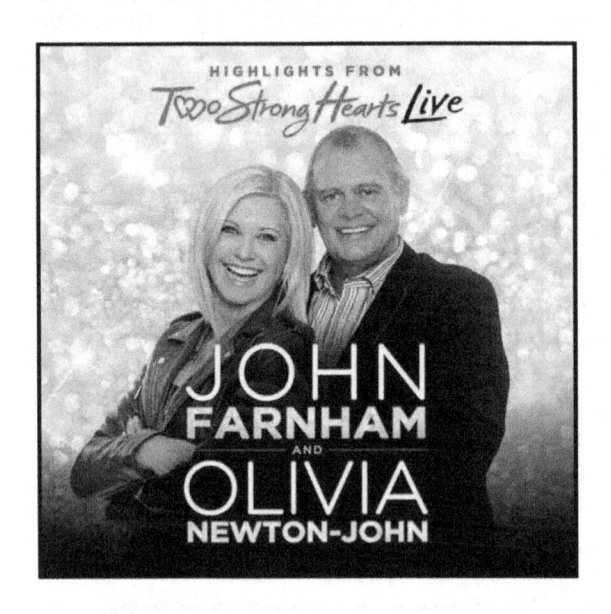

Overture
John & Olivia: *Two Strong Hearts/Let Me Be There*
Olivia: *Xanadu/I Honestly Love You*
John & Olivia: *Tenterfield Saddler*
John: *No One Comes Close/Love To Shine*
John & Olivia: *Suddenly/Dare To Dream/Somewhere Over The Rainbow/Burn For You/ Hit The Road Jack/Fever/You're The One That I Want/Summer Nights/Hearts On Fire/ If Not For You/Every Time You Cry/Physical/You're The Voice/It's A Long Way To The Top (If You Want To Rock 'N Roll)*

Produced by Ross Fraser & Chong Lin.

Australia: Sony Music 88875103742 (2015).

12.07.15: **1-1-1**-6-10-11-20-19-10-11-15-35-39-49-63-76-88-87-89-x-x-93-79-59-63

UK: Not Released.

Following the success of her The Main Event Tour with John Farnham and Anthony Warlow in 1998, Olivia was reunited with Farnham in April 2015, for concerts staged at a number of Australian venues including the Rod Laver Arena in Melbourne,
    During the Two Strong Hearts concerts, accompanied by The Farnham Band & Orchestra, Olivia and John Farnham performed a mix of covers and their respective hits

together, with Farnham duetting with Olivia on songs such as *You're The One That I Want*, *Summer Nights* and *Suddenly*.

A live album titled *HIGHLIGHTS FROM TWO STRONG HEARTS LIVE* was released in June 2015, in Australia only – it made its chart debut at no.1, and held the top spot for an impressive three weeks. A similarly titled home music video was released in August, again only in Australia.

32 ~ FRIENDS FOR CHRISTMAS

Let It Snow! Let It Snow! Let It Snow!/It's Beginning To Look A Lot Like Christmas/Have Yourself A Merry Little Christmas/Santa Claus Is Coming To Town/The Christmas Song/Winter Wonderland/Baby, It's Cold Outside/Silent Night/White Christmas/The Little Drummer Boy/Silver Bells/Hark! The Herald Angels Sing

Deluxe Edition Bonus Tracks: *The First Noel/Here Comes Santa Claus/One Little Christmas Tree*

Produced by Chong Lim.

Australia: Sony Music 88985387172 (2016), Sony Music 88985498012 (Deluxe Edition, 2017).

21.11.16: 3-6-4-4-**1-1**-2-53
26.11.17: 10-8-6-4-5-6 (Deluxe Edition)

FRIENDS FOR CHRISTMAS was Olivia's fifth Christmas album (including one compilation), and came four years after her festive collaboration with John Travolta, *THIS CHRISTMAS*. The album was the third Olivia recorded with John Farnham, and featured versions of a dozen well known Christmas classics. The album was recorded at Playback Recording Studio in Santa Barbara, California.

'It was such a joy singing those beautiful holiday songs with my favourite singer and good mate John Farnham,' said Olivia. 'The holidays are about family and friends, and having this chance to sing these classics with John was pure fun from beginning to end.'

Farnham concurred, saying, 'I have always loved working with Olivia. To record a Christmas album seemed like the right, almost inevitable thing to do. I hope everyone enjoys listening to it as much as we loved recording it together.'

Like Olivia's previous collaborations with John Farnham, *FRIENDS FOR CHRISTMAS* was released exclusively in Australia, where it made its chart debut at no.3. Four weeks later, the album rose to no.1 – Olivia's sixth chart topping album, including the *GREASE* and *XANADU* soundtracks.

Just a month before *FRIENDS FOR CHRISTMAS* appeared, Olivia released another new album, this time in Europe, Japan and North America, as well as Australia. This album, titled *LIV ON*, was a collaboration with Amy Sky and Beth Nielsen Chapman.

'As a group,' said Olivia, 'it's our intention with this album to create songs with a message of compassion and hope.'

LIV ON made its chart debut in Australia at no.72, and slipped out of the chart again the following week. The album was also a minor hit in Ireland and the UK, but failed to chart in most countries where it was released.

A deluxe edition of *FRIENDS FOR CHRISTMAS*, with three bonus tracks, was released a year after the original album. Once again, it was only issued in Australia, where it made its chart debut at no.10 and peaked at no.6.

THE ALMOST TOP 40 ALBUMS

Two of Olivia's albums have made the Top 50 in one or more countries, but failed to enter the Top 40 in any.

WARM AND TENDER

This album of children's lullabies, released in 1989, featured Olivia singing such well-known songs as *Twinkle, Twinkle Little Star*, *Rock-A-Bye Baby*, *Over The Rainbow*, *The Twelfth Of Never* and *When You Wish Upon A Star*. The album charted at no.43 in Japan, and a lowly no.124 in the USA, but it failed to enter the Top 40 anywhere.

ONE WOMAN'S LIVE JOURNEY

This live album was recorded at the Trump Taj Mahal in Atlantic City, New Jersey, during Olivia's concerts on the 26th and 27th August 1999. Only released in Australia and North America, the album missed the chart in Canada and the USA, but rose to no.41 in Australia – just one place short of Top 40 status.

OLIVIA'S TOP 20 ALBUMS

This Top 20 Albums has been compiled using the same points system as for Olivia's Top 25 Singles listing.

Rank/Album/Artist/Points

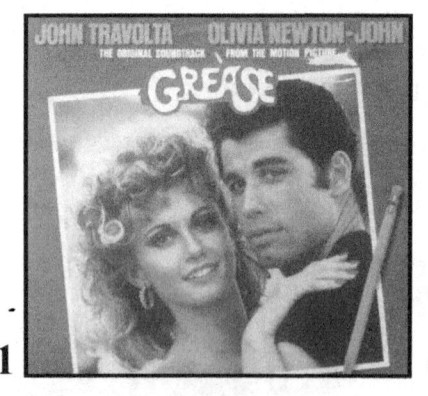

1 *GREASE* – 3594 points

2 *XANADU* – 1806 points

3 *PHYSICAL* – 1092 points

Rank/Album/Artist/Points

4 *TOTALLY HOT* – 848 points

5 *GREATEST HITS VOL.3 / VOL.2* – 786 points

6. *GREATEST HITS / VOL.2* – 673 points
7. *HAVE YOU NEVER BEEN MELLOW* – 601 points
8. *COME ON OVER* – 526 points
9. *SOUL KISS* – 497 points
10. *CLEARLY LOVE* – 374 points

11. *TWO OF A KIND* – 316 points
12. *FIRST IMPRESSIONS – GREAT HITS!* – 302 points
13. *MAKING A GOOD THING BETTER* – 279 points
14. *IF YOU LOVE ME LET ME KNOW* – 269 points
15. *LET ME BE THERE* – 263 points

16. *DON'T STOP BELIEVIN'* – 248 points
17. *BACK TO BASICS – THE ESSENTIAL COLLECTION 1971-1992* – 246 points
18. *GREATEST HITS VOLUME 2* (1977) – 237 points
19. *OLIVIA'S GREATEST HITS* – 192 points
20. *THE RUMOUR* – 163 points

Just as singles from *Grease* dominate the Top 25 Singles list, so the *GREASE* soundtrack tops this Top 20 Albums list, scoring almost twice as many points as its nearest rival, another soundtrack, *XANADU*. Olivia's most successful solo albums are *PHYSICAL* and *TOTALLY HOT*, followed by two greatest hits compilations.

ALBUMS TRIVIA

To date, Olivia has achieved thirty-one Top 40 albums in one or more of the countries featured in this book.

There follows a country-by-country look at Olivia's most successful albums.

OLIVIA IN AUSTRALIA

Olivia has achieved 27 hit albums in Australia, with a total of 633 weeks.

No.1 Albums

1978	*GREASE*
1980	*XANADU*
1982	*GREATEST HITS VOLUME 3*
1998	*HIGHLIGHTS FROM THE MAIN EVENT*
2015	*HIGHLIGHTS FROM TWO STRONG HEARTS LIVE*
2016	*FRIENDS FOR CHRISTMAS*

Most weeks at no.1

11 weeks	*GREASE*
6 weeks	*XANADU*
3 weeks	*HIGHLIGHTS FROM TWO STRONG HEARTS LIVE*

Albums with the most weeks

101 weeks	*GREASE*
75 weeks	*GREATEST HITS VOLUME 2*
46 weeks	*FIRST IMPRESSIONS – GREAT HITS!*
39 weeks	*PHYSICAL*
38 weeks	*GREATEST HITS VOLUME 3*
31 weeks	*XANADU*
28 weeks	*HIGHLIGHTS FROM THE MAIN EVENT*
24 weeks	*LONG LIVE LOVE*
24 weeks	*TWO OF A KIND*
23 weeks	*TOTALLY HOT*
23 weeks	*HIGHLIGHTS FROM TWO STRONG HEARTS LIVE*

ARIA (Australian Recording Industry Association) Accreditations

The current ARIA accreditations are: Gold = 35,000, Platinum = 70,000.

14 x Platinum   *GREASE* (2012) = 980,000
5 x Platinum   *HIGHLIGHTS FROM THE MAIN EVENT* (1999) = 350,000
2 x Platinum   *FRIENDS FOR CHRISTMAS* (2016) = 140,000
2 x Platinum   *FRIENDS FOR CHRISTMAS* (Deluxe Edition) (2018) = 140,000
Platinum   *IF NOT FOR YOU* (?) = 70,000
Platinum   *PHYSICAL* (1982) = 70,000
Platinum   *(2)* (2002) = 70,000
Gold   *INDIGO – WOMEN OF SONG* (2004) = 35,000
Gold   *HIGHLIGHTS FROM TWO STRONG HEARTS LIVE* (2015) = 35,000

Note: this list is incomplete.

OLIVIA IN AUSTRIA

Olivia has only achieved two hit albums in Austria, both soundtracks, and both chart toppers.

GREASE was no.1 for two months on the monthly chart, and *XANADU* was no.1 for a single chart on the bi-weekly chart.

Most weeks on the chart

52 weeks   *GREASE*
24 weeks   *XANADU*

OLIVIA IN CANADA

Olivia has achieved 17 hit albums on Canada's RPM chart, which spent a total of 422 weeks on the chart.

No.1 Albums

1974   *IF YOU LOVE ME LET ME KNOW*
1978   *GREASE*

Most weeks at No.1

7 weeks *GREASE*
1 week   *IF YOU LOVE ME LET ME KNOW*

Albums with the most weeks

73 weeks *GREATEST HITS VOL.2*
42 weeks *GREASE*
41 weeks *IF YOU LOVE ME LET ME KNOW*
38 weeks *HAVE YOU NEVER BEEN MELLOW*
36 weeks *PHYSICAL*
31 weeks *TOTALLY HOT*
28 weeks *XANADU*
21 weeks *CLEARLY LOVE*
21 weeks *TWO OF A KIND*
19 weeks *GREATEST HITS*

Note: no information is available for the Canadian album chart from 2000 to 2015.

Music Canada Album Certifications

Diamond   *GREASE* (November 1978) = 1 million
5 x Platinum   *GREATEST HITS VOL.2* (March 1984) = 500,000
4 x Platinum   *PHYSICAL* (May 1982) = 400,000
2 x Platinum   *HAVE YOU NEVER BEEN MELLOW* (May 1978) – 200,000
2 x Platinum   *XANADU* (March 1982) = 200,000
Platinum   *CLEARLY LOVE* (March 1976) = 100,000
Platinum   *GREATEST HITS* (November 1977) = 100,000
Platinum   *LET ME BE THERE* (November 1977) = 100,000
Platinum   *COME ON OVER* (November 1977) = 100,000
Platinum   *IF YOU LOVE ME LET ME GO* (May 1978) = 100,000
Platinum   *TOTALLY HOT* (December 1978) = 100,000
Gold   *DON'T STOP BELIEVIN'* (February 1977) = 50,000
Gold   *MAKING A GOOD THING BETTER* (October 1977) = 50,000
Gold   *SOUL KISS* (December 1985) = 50,000

OLIVIA IN GERMANY

Olivia has achieved five hit albums in Germany, which have spent a total of 94 weeks on the chart.

No.1 Albums

1978	*GREASE*
1980	*XANADU*

Most weeks at No.1

11 weeks	*GREASE*
1 week	*XANADU*

Most weeks on the chart

37 weeks	*GREASE*
30 weeks	*XANADU*
19 weeks	*PHYSICAL*

OLIVIA IN JAPAN

Olivia has achieved 19 hit albums in Japan, which have spent a total of 505 weeks on the chart.

Only one album, the soundtrack *GREASE*, went to no.1 – it topped the chart for 3 weeks.

Most weeks on the chart

72 weeks	*COME ON OVER*
48 weeks	*HAVE YOU NEVER BEEN MELLOW*
45 weeks	*XANADU*
44 weeks	*LET ME BE THERE*
31 weeks	*PHYSICAL*
30 weeks	*CLEARLY LOVE*
30 weeks	*GREASE*
29 weeks	*GREATEST HITS*
26 weeks	*CRYSTAL LADY*
26 weeks	*DON'T STOP BELIEVIN'*

OLIVIA IN THE NETHERLANDS

Olivia has achieved eight hit albums in the Netherlands, with a total of 197 weeks on the chart.

No.1 Albums

1978	*GREASE*
1980	*XANADU*

GREASE returned to no.1 in 1991.

Most weeks at No.1

14 weeks	*GREASE*
3 weeks	*XANADU*

Most weeks on the chart

110 weeks	*GREASE*
23 weeks	*XANADU*
18 weeks	*GREATEST HITS*
18 weeks	*TOTALLY HOT*
14 weeks	*PHYSICAL*

OLIVIA IN NEW ZEALAND

Olivia has achieved 12 hit albums in New Zealand, which spent a total of 296 weeks on the chart.

Olivia's most successful album, and her only no.1, is the soundtrack *GREASE*, which topped the chart for 16 weeks.

Albums with the most weeks

85 weeks	*GREASE*
81 weeks	*FIRST IMPRESSIONS – GREAT HITS!*
22 weeks	*GREATEST HITS VOL.2*
19 weeks	*GREATEST HITS VOL.3*
18 weeks	*COME ON OVER*

17 weeks   *PHYSICAL*
16 weeks   *XANADU*
13 weeks   *HAVE YOU NEVER BEEN MELLOW*
11 weeks   *TOTALLY HOT*
10 weeks   *BACK TO BASICS – THE ESSENTIAL COLLECTION 1971-1992*

OLIVIA IN NORWAY

Olivia has achieved five hit albums in Norway, which spent a total of 127 weeks on the chart.

No.1 Albums

1978   *GREASE*
1980   *XANADU*

GREASE returned to no.1 in 1998.

Most weeks at No.1

17 weeks   *GREASE*
 9 weeks   *XANADU*

Albums with the most weeks

52 weeks   *GREASE*
32 weeks   *XANADU*
22 weeks   *TOTALLY HOT*
17 weeks   *PHYSICAL*

OLIVIA IN SOUTH AFRICA

Between 1981 and 1995, Olivia achieved two hit albums in South Africa, which spent a total of 22 weeks on the chart.

Her most successful album during this period was *GREATEST HITS VOL.2*, which peaked at no.4.

Albums with the most weeks

13 weeks   *GREATEST HITS VOL.2*
 9 weeks   *PHYSICAL*

OLIVIA IN SPAIN

Olivia has achieved two hit albums in Spain, both soundtracks, which spent a total 122 weeks on the chart.

No.1 Albums

1978   *GREASE*
1980   *XANADU*

GREASE returned to no.1 in 1991.

Most weeks at No.1

19 weeks   *GREASE*
 2 weeks   *XANADU*

Most week on the chart

102 weeks   *GREASE*
 20 weeks   *XANADU*

OLIVIA IN SWEDEN

Olivia has achieved five hit albums in Sweden, which have spent 113 weeks on the chart.

No.1 Albums

1978   *GREASE*
1980   *XANADU*

Most weeks at No.1

16 weeks   *GREASE*

6 weeks   *XANADU*

Most weeks on the chart

49 weeks   *GREASE*
28 weeks   *XANADU*
18 weeks   *TOTALLY HOT*
16 weeks   *PHYSICAL*

OLIVIA IN SWITZERLAND

Only two of Olivia's albums have charted in Switzerland, the soundtracks *GREASE* and *XANADU*.

No.1 Albums

1978   *GREASE*
1980   *XANADU*

Most weeks at No.1

14 weeks   *GREASE*
 2 weeks   *XANADU*

Most weeks on the chart

30 weeks   *GREASE*
22 weeks   *XANADU*

OLIVIA IN THE UK

Olivia has achieved 16 hit albums in the UK, with a total of 187 weeks on the Top 100 chart.

Her most successful album, and her only no.1, is the soundtrack *GREASE*, which topped the chart for 13 weeks.

Albums with the most weeks

46 weeks	*GREASE*
38 weeks	*GREATEST HITS* (1982)
22 weeks	*PHYSICAL*
17 weeks	*XANADU*
14 weeks	*TOTALLY HOT*
13 weeks	*THE DEFINITIVE COLLECTION*
9 weeks	*GREATEST HITS* (1975)

BPI (British Phonographic Industry) Awards

The BPI began certifying albums in 1973, and between April 1973 and December 1978, awards related to a monetary value and not a unit value. Thanks to inflation, this changed several times over the years:

- April 1973 – August 1974: Silver = £75,000, Gold = £150,000, Platinum = £1 million.
- September 1974 – December 1975: Gold raised to £250,000, others unchanged.
- January 1976 – December 1976: Silver raised to £100,000, others unchanged.
- January 1977 – December 1978: Silver raised to £150,000, Gold raised to £300,000, Platinum unchanged.

When this system was abolished, the awards that were set remain in place today: Silver = 60,000, Gold = 100,000, Platinum = 300,000. Multi-Platinum awards were introduced in February 1987.

In July 2013 the BPI automated awards, and awards from this date are based on actual sales since February 1994, not shipments.

8 x Platinum	*GREASE* (February 2016) = 2.4 million
Platinum	*GREATEST HITS* (1982) (February 1983) = 300,000
Gold	*TOTALLY HOT* (January 1979) = 100,000
Gold	*XANADU* (August 1980) = 100,000
Gold	*THE DEFINITIVE COLLECTION* (November 2014) = 100,000
Silver	*GREATEST HITS* (1975) (December 1977) = 60,000
Silver	*PHYSICAL* (April 1982) = 60,000

OLIVIA IN THE USA

Olivia has achieved 17 hit albums in the USA, with a total of 371 weeks on the Top 100 of the Billboard 200 chart.

No.1 Albums

1974	*IF YOU LOVE ME LET ME KNOW*
1975	*HAVE YOU NEVER BEEN MELLOW*
1978	*GREASE*

GREASE topped the Billboard 200 for 12 weeks, and the other two albums for one week each.

Albums with the most weeks

76 weeks	*GREATEST HITS VOL.2*
49 weeks	*GREASE*
32 weeks	*PHYSICAL*
30 weeks	*XANADU*
28 weeks	*IF YOU LOVE ME LET ME KNOW*
28 weeks	*HAVE YOU NEVER BEEN MELLOW*
28 weeks	*TOTALLY HOT*
23 weeks	*DON'T STOP BELIEVIN'*
15 weeks	*COME ON OVER*
15 weeks	*GREATEST HITS*
15 weeks	*TWO OF A KIND*

RIAA (Recording Industry Association of America) Awards

The RIAA began certifying Gold albums in 1958, Platinum albums in 1976, and multi-Platinum albums in 1984. Gold = 500,000, Platinum = 1 million. Awards are based on shipments, not sales, and each disc is counted individually (so, for example, a double album has to ship 500,000 to be eligible for Platinum).

8 x Platinum	*GREASE* (November 1984) = 4 million
2 x Platinum	*XANADU* (October 1984) = 2 million
2 x Platinum	*GREATEST HITS VOL.2* (October 1984) = 2 million
2 x Platinum	*GREATEST HITS* (October 1984) = 2 million
2 x Platinum	*PHYSICAL* (October 1984) = 2 million
Platinum	*TOTALLY HOT* (December 1978) = 1 million

Platinum	*TWO OF A KIND* (January 1984) = 1 million
Gold	*IF YOU LOVE ME LET ME KNOW* (September 1974) = 500,000
Gold	*LET ME BE THERE* (October 1974) = 500,000
Gold	*HAVE YOU NEVER BEEN MELLOW* (February 1975) = 500,000
Gold	*CLEARLY LOVE* (September 1975) = 500,000
Gold	*COME ON OVER* (April 1976) = 500,000
Gold	*DON'T STOP BELIEVIN'* (December 1976) = 500,000
Gold	*SOUL KISS* (December 1985) = 500,000
Gold	*BACK TO BASICS – THE ESSENTAIL COLLECTION 1971-1992* (July 1998) = 500,000

By the same author …

If you have enjoyed *Olivia Newton-John: All The Top 40 Hits*, you may be interested to learn there are four more books in Craig Halstead's Top 40 series, plus a book detailing UK Christmas Number Ones from 1940 to date:

- *Janet Jackson: All The Top 40 Hits*
- *Michael Jackson: All The Top 40 Hits*
- *Carpenters: All The Top 40 Hits*
- *ABBA: All The Top 40 Hits*
- *Christmas Number Ones*

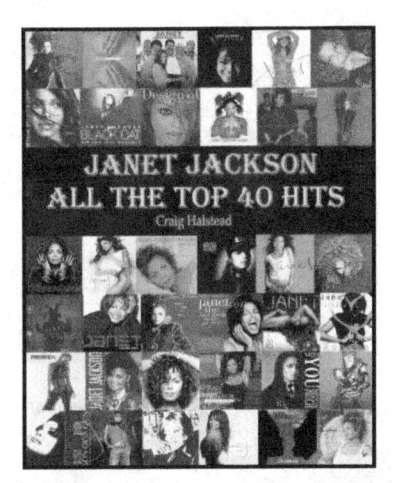

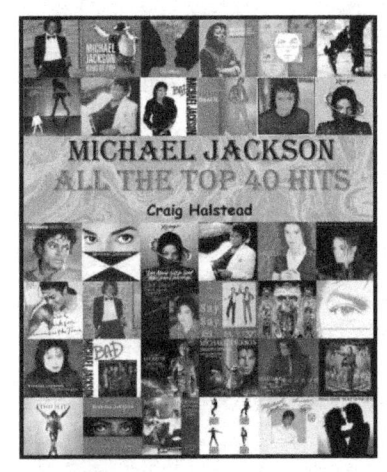

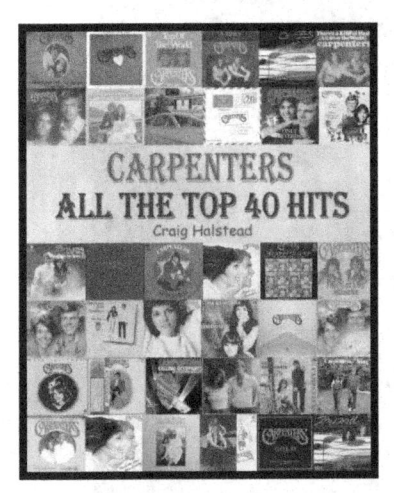

Craig Halstead has also written (or co-written with Chris Cadman), four 'For The Record' books, which look at the careers of Donna Summer, Janet Jackson, Michael Jackson & Whitney Houston in far greater depth, and typically include: The Songs (A-Z of released/unreleased songs), The Albums, TV/Films, The Home Videos, The Concerts, Chartography, USA Discography & UK Discography.

Made in the USA
Middletown, DE
13 March 2019